Unified Cybersecurity SOC 2 Compliance for Startups and SMBs

A Step by Step Strategy

Jose Jesus Nava Rascon

Amazon Kindle Direct Distribution

Copyright © 2024 Jose Jesus Nava Rascon.

All rights reserved. This book or any portion thereof may not be reproduced or used in any manner whatsoever without the express written permission of the author except for the use of brief quotations in a book review.

Printed and distributed by Amazon Kindle Direct.

First printing, 2024.

Jose Jesus Nava Rascon

Table of Contents

Foreword...10

Introduction...13

Chapter 1 Understanding SOC 2 for Our Company..............17

    1.1: Assess and Understand the SOC 2 Trust Services Criteria (TSC) Mapped to the Company Based on Industry Nature, Company Needs, Goals, and Objectives 18

    1.2: Cybersecurity Questions and Templates to Understand What We Need 23

    1.3: Practical Tools for Startups and SMBs.................................27

Chapter 2 Writing Our Information Security Policy.............29

    2.1: Writing the Mission, Vision, and Objectives of SOC 2............30

    2.2: Key Components of an Information Security Policy (ISP) 34

    2.3: Communicating and Implementing the Information Security Policy 39

Chapter 3 Using NIST CSF for a First Assessment of Our Company..42

    3.1: Use NIST Quick Start Guide (QSG) for CSF to Understand: Govern, Identify, Protect, Detect, Respond, Recover 43

    3.2: Overview of NIST CSF 2.0 Core Functions 43

    3.3: Conducting an Assessment with the Govern Function 46

    3.4: Conducting an Assessment with the Identify Function 47

    3.5: Conducting an Assessment with the Protect Function..............49

    3.6: Conducting an Assessment with the Detect Function................50

    3.7: Conducting an Assessment with the Respond Function 51

    3.8: Conducting an Assessment with the Recover Function.............52

    3.9: Documenting the NIST CSF 2.0 Assessment Findings 53

Chapter 4 Mapping Our Company's NIST CSF Assessment to SOC 2 Trust Services Criteria (TSCs) 55

    4.1: Overview of the NIST CSF and SOC 2 TSCs 56

4.2: Mapping the Govern Function to SOC 2 TSCs 59

4.3: Mapping the Identify Function to SOC 2 TSCs 60

4.4: Mapping the Protect Function to SOC 2 TSCs 61

4.5: Mapping the Detect Function to SOC 2 TSCs 62

4.6: Mapping the Respond Function to SOC 2 TSCs 63

4.7: Mapping the Recover Function to SOC 2 TSCs 64

4.8: Practical Steps for Mapping NIST CSF 2.0 to SOC 2 TSCs 66

Chapter 5 Creating a NIST CSF Current Profile for Our Company 68

5.1: Purpose and Benefits of a Current Profile 69

5.2: Assessing the Govern Function for the Current Profile 69

5.3: Assessing the Identify Function for the Current Profile 71

5.4: Assessing the Protect Function for the Current Profile 72

5.5: Assessing the Detect Function for the Current Profile 73

5.6: Assessing the Respond Function for the Current Profile 74

5.7: Assessing the Recover Function for the Current Profile 75

5.8: Documenting the Current Profile and Preparing for Future Improvements 77

Chapter 6 Creating a NIST CSF 2.0 Target Profile for Our Company 79

6.1: Purpose and Benefits of a Target Profile 80

6.2: Defining the Target Profile for the Govern Function 80

6.3: Defining the Target Profile for the Identify Function 82

6.4: Defining the Target Profile for the Protect Function 83

.... 84

6.5: Defining the Target Profile for the Detect Function 84

6.6: Defining the Target Profile for the Respond Function 86

6.7: Defining the Target Profile for the Recover Function 87

6.8: Documenting the Target Profile and Setting Goals for Future .. 88

Chapter 7 Assessing NIST CSF 2.0 Tiers for Use in Current and Target Profiles 90

7.1: Understanding the Purpose and Benefits of NIST CSF 2.0 Tiers 91

7.2: Tier 1 – Partial 92

7.3: Tier 2 – Risk Informed 93

7.4: Tier 3 – Repeatable 94

7.5: Tier 4 – Adaptive 96

7.6: Selecting a Target Tier for Your Organization 97

7.7: Documenting the Current and Target Tier Assessments ... 98

Chapter 8 Analyzing the Gaps Between our NIST CSF 2.0 Current and Target Profiles 100

8.1: Purpose and Benefits of a Gap Analysis 101

8.2: Analyzing Gaps in the Govern Function 101

8.3: Analyzing Gaps in the Identify Function 102

8.4: Analyzing Gaps in the Protect Function 104

8.5: Analyzing Gaps in the Detect Function 105

8.6: Analyzing Gaps in the Respond Function 106

8.7: Analyzing Gaps in the Recover Function 107

8.8: Prioritizing and Documenting the Gap Analysis Findings 109

Chapter 9 Understanding Why Configuration Management is the Center of the Universe 111

9.1: Where Everything Unveils – The Importance of Configuration Management 112

9.2: Creating a Configuration Management Strategy 114

9.3: The Relationship Between Configuration Management and Other Key Security Practices 118

9.4: Configuration Management Best Practices for Startups and SMBs 121

Chapter 10 Understanding Hardening 124

5

10.1: Physical Security – Setting Environment Controls Around Secure and Controlled Locations 125

10.2: Operating Systems – Ensuring Patches Are Deployed and Access to Firmware is Locked 126

10.3: Applications – Establishing Rules on Installing Software and Default Configurations 128

10.4: Security Appliances – Ensuring Anti-Virus is Deployed and Any End-Point Protections are Reporting Appropriately 129

10.5: Networks and Services – Removing Unnecessary Services (e.g., Telnet, FTP) and Enabling Secure Protocols (e.g., SSH, SFTP) 131

10.6: System Auditing and Monitoring – Enabling Traceability and Monitoring of Events 132

10.7: Access Control – Ensuring Default Accounts Are Renamed or Disabled 134

10.8: Data Encryption – Encryption Ciphers to Use (e.g., SHA-256) 135

10.9: Patching and Updates – Ensuring Patches and Updates are Successfully Being Deployed 136

10.10: System Backup – Ensuring Backups are Properly Configured 137

Chapter 11 Our Company Path to Vulnerability Management *139*

11.1: Attack Surfaces and Attack Vectors 140

11.2: Risk Management 141

11.3: Data Classification 143

11.4: Data Retention 144

11.5: Incident Management 145

11.6: Business Continuity and Disaster Recovery 147

11.7: Commercial Tools That Can Ease the Burden 148

11.8: Building a Comprehensive Vulnerability Management Program 150

Chapter 12 Creating Our Company's Action Plan to Achieve Our Target State *152*

    12.1: Inventory of Cybersecurity Policies.................................153

    12.2: Inventory of Policies and SOPs Related to Cybersecurity Assessment..155

    12.3: Information Security Management 156

    12.4: Asset Management..157

    12.5: Access Management 159

    12.6: Data Classification 161

    12.7: Data Retention 162

    12.8: Incident Management..163

    12.9: Configuration Management 164

    12.10: Release Management 165

    12.11: Project Management 166

    12.12: Understanding How the Company Can Leverage a SOC 2 Report from a Cloud Vendor 167

    12.13: Understanding Risk Management from Third-Party Vendors and What to Assess 168

    12.14: Updating Current Policies and SOPs 169

    12.15: Creating New Needed Policies and SOPs.....................169

Chapter 13 Navigating the Most Common Challenges and Tradeoffs to Reach Our Target State Faster *171*

    13.1: Strategies for Maximizing the Few Roles in Startups and SMBs 172

    13.2: Role Multiplicity and Cross-Training..............................174

    13.3: Automation and Tool Utilization 175

    13.4: Prioritization and Risk-Based Approach 177

    13.5: Outsourcing and Consultants...178

    13.6: Documentation and Standardization................................180

    13.7: Regular Training and Awareness....................................182

13.8: Effective Communication and Collaboration 183

13.9: Scalable Solutions 184

Chapter 14 SOC 2 and ISO 27001 Intersections................... 187

14.1: Understanding the Differences Between SOC 2 and ISO 27001 188

14.2: Overlapping Security Controls Between SOC 2 and ISO 27001 190

14.3: Aligning SOC 2 and ISO 27001 Compliance Efforts 193

14.4: Practical Example of Combining SOC 2 and ISO 27001 196

14.5: Common Pitfalls and How to Avoid Them 197

Chapter 15 Checklists and Templates to Get Ready for Audits 199

15.1: Why Checklists and Templates are Crucial for Audit Preparation 200

15.2: SOC 2 Audit Readiness Checklist 201

15.3: Evidence Collection Template 205

15.4: Policy Templates for Audit Preparation 207

15.5: Ongoing Audit Readiness and Maintenance........... 209

Chapter 16 Our SOC 2 Readiness Assessment...................... 212

16.1: What is a Readiness Assessment?.......................... 213

16.2: How to Find the Best Company to Work With..... 215

16.3: Understanding Our Findings................................... 217

16.4: Creating an Action Plan 219

16.5: Post-Readiness Assessment Best Practices........... 222

Chapter 17 Getting Ready for Our SOC 2 Audit................... 225

17.1: Understanding the SOC 2 Audit Process 226

17.2: Final Preparations Before the Audit 227

17.3: Engaging with Auditors During the Audit............. 229

17.4: Navigating the Audit Findings and Report 230

17.5: Maintaining Compliance After the Audit 232

Conclusion..*235*
Bibliography *238*

Foreword

In today's digital age, cybersecurity has evolved from a niche concern to a cornerstone of trust and business continuity for organizations of all sizes. Whether you're a startup forging a path toward growth or an established small or medium-sized business (SMB) navigating client compliance demands and an expanding market, securing your systems, data, and services is critical, not only to protect your assets but also to meet the rising expectations of your customers and partners, then this book is for you. The journey to establishing and maintaining a robust security posture can seem daunting, especially for companies with limited resources and expertise. This is where compliance frameworks like **SOC 2** come into play, offering a structured pathway to securing information systems and proving to the world that your organization can be trusted. But for many startups and SMBs, achieving SOC 2 compliance is a challenging endeavor, often hindered by budget constraints, a lack of dedicated security staff, and the overwhelming nature of cybersecurity itself.

This book, *"Unified Cybersecurity SOC 2 Compliance for Startups and SMBs: A Step by Step Strategy"*, was born out of the necessity to simplify this process. It is designed to guide business leaders, CTOs, IT managers, and security professionals through the complexities of SOC 2 compliance in a practical, accessible way. More than just another technical manual, this book bridges the gap between industry best practices and the real-world constraints faced by startups and SMBs. It offers actionable strategies, checklists, and templates to help you not only achieve SOC 2 compliance but also to build a sustainable cybersecurity program that aligns with your business objectives.

What sets this book apart is its focus on balancing technical rigor with practicality. Understanding that many organizations do not have the luxury of unlimited budgets, large cybersecurity teams, it emphasizes the use of automation, smart outsourcing, and role multiplicity to make security achievable without sacrificing growth. The book also integrates globally recognized frameworks like the **NIST Cybersecurity Framework (CSF)** on its latest version v2.0, released on February 2024, and **ISO 27001**, highlighting intersections with SOC 2 to help organizations streamline their efforts and address multiple compliance requirements simultaneously.

As we move forward in an increasingly interconnected and data-driven world, where AI and parallel computing advances threaten any company's security posture, the need for robust cybersecurity practices will only grow. Customers demand transparency and assurance that their data is safe, partners expect reliable security measures, and regulatory requirements continue to evolve. This book equips startups and SMBs with the tools, knowledge, and confidence to meet those challenges head-on, allowing you to protect your business while remaining agile and competitive in today's market.

I invite you to embark on this journey, knowing that you have in your hands a guide that not only simplifies the complexity of SOC 2 compliance but also empowers you to build a culture of security within your organization.

Whether you are starting from scratch or refining an existing security program or strategy, this book will serve as your roadmap to achieving both compliance and peace of mind.

Welcome to your cybersecurity journey.

Introduction

In today's fast-paced digital landscape, cybersecurity is no longer an optional consideration for startups and small-to-medium-sized businesses (SMBs); it's a critical component of survival and growth. As cyber threats grow in frequency and sophistication (we know the challenges GenAI and Quantum Computing bringing to the table in terms of cybersecurity impacts), and as regulatory requirements expand, these businesses face unique challenges in safeguarding their data, protecting customer trust, and maintaining compliance with security standards. However, establishing robust cybersecurity practices can be overwhelming, especially for organizations that may lack the resources or expertise of larger enterprises.

For startups and SMBs, the journey to secure their information systems while meeting regulatory requirements like SOC 2 compliance often feels like navigating a maze. SOC 2, which ensures that companies implement appropriate controls to protect data and systems, is increasingly required by customers and partners. Yet, it can seem complex and unattainable, particularly for organizations juggling limited time, personnel, roles, and budgets.

This book, *"Unified Cybersecurity SOC 2 Compliance for Startups and SMBs: A Step by Step Strategy"*, is designed to simplify that journey. It serves as a practical guide for new businesses and smaller enterprises looking to achieve SOC 2 compliance while integrating broader industry standards, such as the NIST Cybersecurity Framework (CSF) and ISO 27001. These frameworks are widely respected, and by aligning them with SOC 2, companies can not only meet compliance requirements but also build a resilient security foundation that scales as their business grows.

The purpose of this book is to demystify the complexity of SOC 2 compliance and provide a comprehensive roadmap for startups and SMBs. It walks through each step of the compliance process, from assessing where your company stands today to identifying gaps, implementing necessary controls, and managing the audit process. Importantly, this guide also addresses the realities of limited resources. It offers strategies for managing trade-offs, automating processes, and making informed decisions that balance security, cost, and efficiency. In doing so, it helps companies prioritize and focus on what matters most, building a secure, compliant infrastructure that supports their growth and customer trust.

Throughout the book, you'll find practical advice, actionable steps, and customizable templates to streamline your compliance journey. Whether you're just starting to think about SOC 2 or you're in the process of preparing for an audit, this book is tailored to meet you where you are. By following the guidance here, you'll not only achieve SOC 2 compliance but also position your organization to handle future cybersecurity challenges with confidence.

Startups and SMBs have the agility to adapt quickly, but they also face pressures to do more with less. The strategies presented in this book leverage that agility while addressing the real-world constraints you face. By focusing on smart, scalable security practices, this guide will empower you to build a cybersecurity program that grows with your business and supports your long-term success.

The following roadmap provides a high-level, visual guide to help you understand the overall process, from initial assessments to audit readiness, with practical milestones along the way. Each step is designed to build a comprehensive and scalable cybersecurity program aligned with both **NIST CSF 2.0** and **SOC 2 Trust Services Criteria (TSC)**, supporting your business in becoming a secure and compliant organization.

Figure 1. Unified SOC 2 Implementation Roadmap

This roadmap serves as your strategic guide, helping you approach each stage methodically and with purpose. Starting from understanding the foundational principles of SOC 2 and NIST CSF, it moves through developing and assessing your organization's cybersecurity posture, implementing controls, and finally preparing for a successful audit. Refer back to this visual at any point to stay aligned with the path to compliance and ensure each milestone brings you closer to a resilient and trustworthy security framework.

In the chapters that follow, you'll learn how to:

- Understand the core principles of SOC 2 compliance and how it applies to your business.
- Leverage industry standards like NIST CSF and ISO 27001 to streamline compliance efforts.
- Build and implement the necessary security controls without overwhelming your resources.
- Navigate common challenges, make trade-offs, and prioritize efforts to get to your compliance goals faster.
- Prepare for SOC 2 audits with practical checklists, templates, and action plans.

The road to compliance may seem daunting, but with the right approach, it's entirely achievable, even for startups and SMBs. This book is your roadmap to success. Let's get started.

Chapter 1

Understanding SOC 2 for Our Company

This chapter introduces SOC 2 and guides startups and SMBs through the foundational steps needed to understand how SOC 2 compliance fits within their business operations. It emphasizes the importance of aligning SOC 2 Trust Services Criteria (TSCs) with company-specific goals, needs, and industry requirements, providing practical steps to kick-start the process.

1.1: Assess and Understand the SOC 2 Trust Services Criteria (TSC) Mapped to the Company Based on Industry Nature, Company Needs, Goals, and Objectives

1.1.1: Overview of SOC 2 Trust Services Criteria (TSCs)

This is where everything starts. SOC 2 compliance focuses on five Trust Services Criteria (TSCs), established by the American Institute of Certified Public Accountants (AICPA). These criteria are central to building and maintaining trust with clients and customers:

SOC 2 Trust Services Criteria

Figure 2. SOC 2 Trust Services Criteria

- **Security**: Protection of information and systems from unauthorized access.

- **Availability**: Ensuring that systems are operational and accessible as agreed upon.
- **Processing Integrity**: Ensuring systems operate as intended, delivering accurate and timely results.
- **Confidentiality**: Protecting sensitive information from unauthorized disclosure.
- **Privacy**: Ensuring that personal information is collected, used, retained, disclosed, and disposed of in compliance with the entity's privacy notice.

These criteria form the backbone of SOC 2 compliance and are used to assess whether a company's systems and processes effectively manage the risks associated with data security, availability, and privacy.

1.1.2: Industry-Specific Mapping of SOC 2 TSCs

Understanding which TSCs apply to your business is crucial and often depends on the nature of your industry and the services provided. A startup operating in financial technology (fintech), for example, may place a higher emphasis on confidentiality and processing integrity due to regulatory pressures around customer data and transaction processing. In contrast, a SaaS company offering a web-based platform might focus more on **security** and **availability** to ensure its service remains operational and safe from threats.

- **Example: Fintech**: Prioritize Confidentiality, Privacy, and Security, as financial data is highly sensitive.
- **Example: SaaS Platforms**: Emphasize Security and Availability, ensuring users can access the service securely and reliably.
- **Example: Healthcare**: Focus on Privacy and Confidentiality, particularly to comply with regulations like HIPAA.

1.1.3: The COSO Framework and SOC 2

The **COSO** (Committee of Sponsoring Organizations of the Treadway Commission) framework is a widely recognized model for designing, implementing, and evaluating internal controls, especially related to financial reporting. It provides a comprehensive system for managing risk, ensuring compliance, and improving organizational performance through five core components: control environment, risk assessment, control activities, information and communication, and monitoring activities. The Common Criteria in SOC 2, which are part of the Trust Services Criteria (TSC), are heavily influenced by the COSO framework. SOC 2 builds on COSO's structure to address the security, availability, confidentiality, processing integrity, and privacy aspects of service organizations, which are essential for safeguarding data in the digital age.

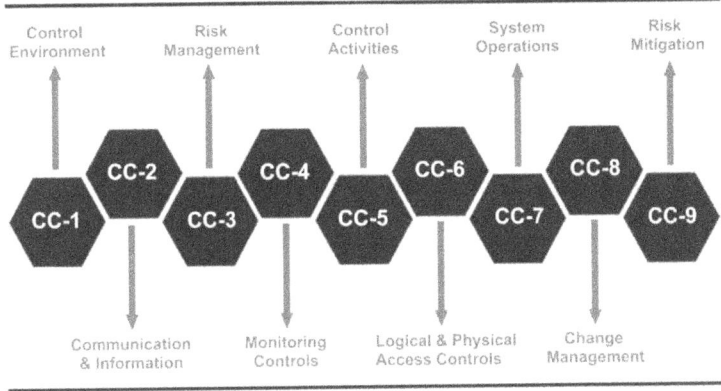

Figure 3. SOC 2 Trust Services Criteria

The Common Criteria within SOC 2 align with COSO's core components by requiring organizations to establish controls related to governance, risk assessment, and control activities, thus ensuring that both internal control and cybersecurity requirements are met. By leveraging COSO's well-established framework, SOC 2 helps organizations create a solid foundation for managing risk, security, and compliance effectively.

1.1.4: Aligning SOC 2 with Company Needs and Future Goals

Once the key TSCs for your industry have been identified, it's important to align them with the company's current needs and future objectives. This ensures SOC 2 compliance supports your business strategy, and is not just a checkbox exercise.

- **Current Needs**: What are your immediate security and compliance concerns? Examples might include the need for better data encryption, enhanced monitoring, or streamlined access controls.
- **Future Goals**: What are your strategic goals for the next 1-3 years? For example:
    - **Scaling**: How does compliance support scalability? As you onboard more clients or move into new markets, how will SOC 2 ensure smooth growth?
    - **Customer Trust**: Many clients demand SOC 2 reports as a baseline for doing business. Achieving compliance can open doors to new opportunities.

1.1.5: Conducting an Initial SOC 2 Gap Analysis

To map your company's current state against SOC 2 requirements, you can begin with a basic **gap analysis**. This process identifies areas where your existing policies, procedures, and technologies may not fully align with SOC 2 TSCs.

- **Step-by-Step Gap Analysis**:

1. **Inventory existing security controls**: Document current systems, processes, and policies.
2. **Identify areas of weakness**: Compare your controls against SOC 2 TSCs. Are there areas where your company doesn't have adequate safeguards?
3. **Document improvement areas**: Highlight specific areas for development or improvement, such as missing encryption policies, lack of access control, or incomplete disaster recovery plans.

In Chapter 8: "Analyzing the Gaps Between our NIST CSF Current and Target Profiles", we will dig deeper into the SOC 2 Gap Analysis, once we have created a NIST Cybersecurity Framework's Current and Target Profiles based on the SOC 2 needs we have, and where we are starting.

1.2: Cybersecurity Questions and Templates to Understand What We Need

1.2.1: Key Questions to Assess SOC 2 Needs

Before diving into a full SOC 2 readiness project, it's essential to ask the right questions to understand where your company stands and what specific needs must be addressed.

These questions help clarify your objectives, risk landscape, and initial priorities.

- **General Security**:
    - What types of data are we handling (e.g., customer PII, financial information, health records)?
    - Do we have documented security policies, and are they being enforced?
    - What access controls are in place to ensure only authorized users can access sensitive data?
- **Have we implemented an Information Asset Classification Program. We need to know what to protect:**
    - **Information Asset Classification Goals:**
        - Provide structural basis for protection efforts. Should be classified based on the value to the organization. A company should never spend more in protecting an asset than the value this asset is giving to the company. Factors of asset classification are determine the relative:
            - **Criticality**
            - **Sensitivity**
        - For each Cloud or On-Premise asset. All together, are the business value.

- **Risk Management**:
    - Have we performed a formal risk assessment to identify our primary cybersecurity risks?
    - How are these risks currently mitigated, and do we have a defined risk management process?
- **Data Availability**:
    - How critical is system uptime for our business? What service level agreements (SLAs) do we have with customers?
    - What measures are in place to ensure system availability (e.g., redundancy, backups, failover procedures)?
- **Incident Response**:
    - Do we have a documented incident response plan? Has it been tested?
    - How do we detect security incidents, and what is our process for responding to them?

1.2.2: SOC 2 Compliance Readiness Questionnaire Template

A simple questionnaire can help your team assess its initial SOC 2 readiness. This document can be distributed across departments (IT, Legal, Operations, etc.) to gather insights into current practices.

Example Questions:

1. **Data Handling**:
   - What types of data does your department handle that would be relevant to SOC 2 (e.g., PII, financial data)?
   - Are there any existing data security policies or controls in place for handling this data?
2. **System Access and Control**:
   - Who has access to critical systems, and how is access managed (e.g., multi-factor authentication, role-based access control)?
   - How often are access rights reviewed, and how are they revoked for former employees or contractors?
3. **Risk Management and Incident Response**:
   - Has the team conducted any formal risk assessments in the past 12 months? If so, what were the key findings?
   - Does the department have an incident response plan? If yes, when was it last tested?
4. **System Availability**:
   - What is the expected uptime for critical systems, and how do you ensure these systems remain available during outages?
   - Are there backup and disaster recovery procedures in place, and how often are they tested?

1.2.3: Example Template for Initial Internal Audit

The internal audit template helps gather data on how well the company currently aligns with SOC 2 criteria. This can serve as a living document, updated as improvements are made.

Sample Sections:

- **Security**: What security measures are in place to protect data?
- **Availability**: What mechanisms are used to ensure continuous system availability?
- **Confidentiality**: How is sensitive data protected, both at rest and in transit?
- **Privacy**: How are personal data processing practices documented and enforced?

1.3: Practical Tools for Startups and SMBs

1.3.1: Tools and Platforms for Initial SOC 2 Preparation

For startups and SMBs, cost-effective tools are essential for implementing SOC 2 controls without large budgets or dedicated security teams. Consider using:

- **Risk Assessment Tools**: Services like **RiskWatch** or **LogicGate** provide structured risk assessments that can align with SOC 2 requirements.
- **Policy Management**: Affordable platforms like **Confluence**, **Jira**, or **Notion** can be used to maintain and share security policies.
- **Cloud Security**: For companies using cloud platforms (AWS, Azure, Google Cloud), leverage built-in compliance and security features to simplify audit preparation (e.g., AWS Config for tracking configuration changes).

1.3.2: Using External SOC 2 Consultants and Advisors

While many startups may not have a dedicated compliance team, external SOC 2 consultants or advisors can provide guidance. Outsourcing certain SOC 2 preparation tasks, such as risk assessments or security policy reviews, can help alleviate the burden on internal teams.

Benefits:

- Access to expertise and resources beyond internal capabilities.
- Accelerating the readiness process with proven frameworks.
- Guidance on industry-specific best practices.

Chapter 2

Writing Our Information Security Policy

This chapter focuses on creating a comprehensive, customized Information Security Policy (ISP) for startups and SMBs seeking SOC 2 compliance. It walks readers through establishing the company's security mission, vision, and objectives, all within the context of the Trust Services Criteria (TSCs). By the end of this chapter, readers will have a clear understanding of how to articulate a security vision that aligns with business goals, regulatory requirements, and SOC 2 principles.

2.1: Writing the Mission, Vision, and Objectives of SOC 2

2.1.1: Defining the Mission of SOC 2 Compliance

What is a Mission Statement? A mission statement provides a concise summary of why information security is important to your organization and the value it delivers to your customers, stakeholders, and business as a whole. In the context of SOC 2, the mission should focus on building trust through security, availability, and privacy.

Example Mission Statement for a Startup or SMB: "Our mission is to ensure the confidentiality, integrity, and availability of customer data by maintaining a robust information security posture that supports our business operations, complies with regulatory standards, and fosters trust with our clients and partners."

- **Confidentiality**: Ensuring sensitive customer and internal data is protected from unauthorized access.
- **Integrity**: Protecting the accuracy and consistency of data throughout its lifecycle.
- **Availability**: Maintaining uptime and accessibility of services as required by customers and business needs.

Steps to Create Your Mission Statement:

1. **Identify key security commitments**: What promises do you make to customers regarding data protection?
2. **Link security to business outcomes**: How does maintaining security help you meet your business goals (e.g., securing customer trust, facilitating growth)?
3. **Keep it concise**: Focus on simplicity. The mission statement should be easily understood by all stakeholders, from technical teams to non-technical staff.

2.1.2: Establishing the Vision for Information Security

What is a Vision Statement? The vision statement outlines the long-term goals for your information security program. It represents the ideal state that your company aspires to achieve as it grows and evolves, particularly in relation to SOC 2 compliance.

Example Vision Statement for a Startup or SMB: "To build and maintain a scalable, proactive information security framework that not only meets current SOC 2 compliance requirements but also anticipates future security risks, ensuring sustainable protection of customer data and operational resilience."

- **Scalability**: As the business grows, so should the security controls, ensuring they can handle increased data, traffic, and complexity.
- **Proactivity**: The focus on being ahead of potential threats by regularly reviewing and updating security measures.
- **Continuous Improvement**: A security program is never static. The vision should aim for continuous evaluation and improvement of the company's security posture.

Steps to Craft Your Vision:

1. **Consider your long-term security goals**: How will security evolve as your business grows? What role will it play in maintaining customer trust and regulatory compliance?
2. **Link the vision to company growth**: Show how security supports future expansions, new product offerings, or entering new markets.
3. **Incorporate innovation and adaptability**: The vision should reflect an adaptable approach to security, anticipating future challenges in cybersecurity.

2.1.3: Defining Information Security Objectives

What Are Security Objectives? Security objectives are specific, measurable goals that your information security program aims to achieve. These should align with the SOC 2 Trust Services Criteria and be designed to support your mission and vision.

Example Objectives for a Startup or SMB:

1. **Protect Customer Data**: Implement encryption, multi-factor authentication, and regular security audits to ensure the confidentiality of customer data.
2. **Ensure System Availability**: Achieve 99.9% uptime by implementing redundant systems, regular backups, and disaster recovery plans.
3. **Improve Incident Response Time**: Reduce the time to detect and respond to security incidents to under 24 hours by leveraging monitoring tools and creating an incident response team.
4. **Maintain Regulatory Compliance**: Ensure compliance with SOC 2, and periodically review other relevant frameworks such as ISO27001, GDPR, or HIPAA based on your industry.

Steps to Create Your Objectives:

1. **Map objectives to TSCs**: For example, if **Availability** is a priority, create objectives around system uptime, resilience, and disaster recovery.

2. **Ensure objectives are SMART (Specific, Measurable, Achievable, Relevant, Time-bound)**: Each objective should be actionable and trackable.
    - Example: Instead of "improve system security," a SMART objective would be: "Implement multi-factor authentication for all privileged accounts within 6 months."
3. **Prioritize based on risk**: Focus on the most critical areas first, such as securing customer data or improving monitoring for threat detection.

2.2: Key Components of an Information Security Policy (ISP)

Your information security policy is a central document outlining how the company will achieve its security objectives. It serves as a guide for employees, contractors, and vendors to understand their role in maintaining security.

2.2.1: Core Sections of an Information Security Policy

An effective Information Security Policy should cover all areas relevant to SOC 2 compliance. Here are the key sections that should be included:

1. **Purpose and Scope**:
    - **Purpose**: The rationale for the policy (e.g., to protect customer data, ensure system availability).

- **Scope**: Who the policy applies to (e.g., all employees, contractors, third-party vendors) and what systems, data, and processes are covered.
2. **Example**: "This policy applies to all employees, contractors, and third-party vendors who access company systems and data. It covers all information technology assets, including networks, databases, software applications, and devices used within the company."
3. **Roles and Responsibilities**:
   - Assign specific security responsibilities across the company, including executive leadership, IT staff, and other employees.
   - **Example Roles**:
     - **CISO (or equivalent)**: Responsible for overall information security strategy.
     - **IT Team**: Implements technical controls and ensures system uptime.
     - **All Employees**: Expected to follow security guidelines (e.g., using strong passwords, reporting suspicious activity).
4. **Security Controls**:
   - Outline the specific security measures in place to protect the company's assets.
   - **Example Security Controls**:

- **Access Control**: Define how access to systems and data is restricted (e.g., role-based access, least privilege).
- **Data Encryption**: Specify encryption standards for data at rest and in transit (e.g., AES-256).
- **Physical Security**: Describe physical measures to protect IT infrastructure (e.g., secure data centers, locked server rooms).

5. **Incident Response Plan**:
   - Include a brief description of the company's approach to detecting, reporting, and responding to security incidents.
   - **Example**: "In the event of a security incident, the incident response team will be notified immediately, and an investigation will be conducted within 24 hours. Incident reports will be filed, and corrective actions will be taken to prevent recurrence."

6. **Data Classification and Protection**:
   - Define how data is classified (e.g., confidential, public, internal use) and the corresponding protection measures.
   - **Example**: "Confidential data, including customer financial information, must be encrypted in transit and at rest, with access restricted to authorized personnel only."

7. **Monitoring and Auditing**:
   - Explain how security controls are monitored and how compliance with the policy will be verified.
   - **Measurement requires identification and tracking of metrics relevant to the task. Among the metrics commonly recommended for a cybersecurity program are:**
     - The time it takes to detect and report security-related incidents
     - The number and frequency of subsequently discovered unreported incidents
     - Comparisons with the cost-effectiveness of peer organizations based on benchmarks
     - The effectiveness of particular controls within their intended use cases
     - Reports indicating security objectives are not being met
     - The durations of time that show an absence of unexpected or undetected security events
     - Quantities and severities of known organizational vulnerabilities

- Consistency of LOG review practices over time
- Percentages of critical processes that have identified continuity objectives and plans
- Results of business continuity (BC) and disaster recovery (DR) tests
- The extent to which key controls are monitored
- The percentage of metrics achieving defined criteria (MetaMetrics)
    - **Example**: "Security logs will be reviewed weekly by the IT team, and annual internal audits will be conducted to assess compliance with this policy."

8. **Policy Enforcement and Disciplinary Actions**:
    - Clearly state the consequences of non-compliance.
    - **Example**: "Employees found to be in violation of this policy may face disciplinary actions up to and including termination of employment."

2.2.2: Developing Customized Security Policies for Startups and SMBs

For startups and SMBs, the policy should be practical, achievable, and designed to evolve as the company grows. Key considerations include:

- **Keep It Simple and Scalable**: Avoid overly complex language or procedures that could overwhelm your small team. The policy should be flexible enough to adapt as the company expands.
- **Leverage Existing Frameworks**: Many startups lack the resources to build policies from scratch. Use existing SOC 2 templates or adopt elements from recognized standards like NIST CSF or ISO 27001.
- **Example Customization**: A startup might focus more on cloud security and remote work policies, while a manufacturing SMB might emphasize physical security and supply chain integrity.

2.3: Communicating and Implementing the Information Security Policy

2.3.1: Policy Communication and Training

Even the most well-written security policies are ineffective if employees don't understand or follow them. A strong communication and training plan is essential.

- **Onboarding**: Ensure new hires are introduced to the security policy as part of their onboarding process.
- **Ongoing Training**: Conduct regular security awareness training to keep employees up-to-date on evolving threats and best practices (e.g., phishing, password hygiene).
- **Leadership Involvement**: Leadership should visibly support the policy, setting the tone for the company's security culture.

Example Training Plan:

- **Quarterly Security Updates**: Send email newsletters with security tips and updates on policy changes.
- **Annual Security Training**: Require all employees to complete an annual security training course that covers the essentials of SOC 2 and the company's security policies.

2.3.2: Reviewing and Updating the Policy

As your company grows and new security threats emerge, it's important to review and update the information security policy regularly.

- **Periodic Reviews**: Set a schedule (e.g., every 6-12 months) for reviewing the policy to ensure it

remains aligned with business needs, new threats, and regulatory changes.
- **Post-Incident Updates**: After any security incidents or audits, review the policy to determine if updates or improvements are needed.

Checklist for Policy Review:

1. Are all security roles and responsibilities still relevant?
2. Have there been any changes in the regulatory environment that impact the policy?
3. Have there been any changes in business operations or IT infrastructure (e.g., new cloud services)?

Chapter 3

Using NIST CSF for a First Assessment of Our Company

This chapter provides a practical guide to conducting an initial cybersecurity assessment using the updated **NIST Cybersecurity Framework (CSF) 2.0**. By leveraging the six core functions of CSF 2.0: **Govern, Identify, Protect, Detect, Respond, and Recover**, your organization can establish a foundational understanding of its cybersecurity strengths, gaps, and areas for improvement. This assessment is critical for determining readiness for **SOC 2 compliance** and helps you prioritize actions that will align your security practices with regulatory requirements. Each function within NIST CSF 2.0 is examined in detail, with actionable steps for assessing your current state in relation to the SOC 2 Trust Services Criteria (TSC).

3.1: Use NIST Quick Start Guide (QSG) for CSF to Understand: Govern, Identify, Protect, Detect, Respond, Recover

This section explains the five core functions of the NIST CSF, providing an actionable roadmap for assessing and improving your company's security posture. We will use the **NIST CSF Quick Start Guide (QSG)**, a simplified resource that helps organizations implement the framework efficiently, to break down the steps you should follow.

3.2: Overview of NIST CSF 2.0 Core Functions

3.2.1: Understanding the Purpose of NIST CSF 2.0

The **NIST CSF 2.0** provides a structured approach to managing cybersecurity risk that has been updated to reflect evolving threats and industry practices. By introducing the **Govern** function and refining other core functions, CSF 2.0 offers a more comprehensive framework for organizations to understand and manage cybersecurity risks, enhance resilience, and improve governance practices.

3.2.2: Core Functions of NIST CSF 2.0

NIST CSF 2.0's six core functions: Govern, Identify, Protect, Detect, Respond, and Recover, each represent critical areas of cybersecurity management. Together, they provide a holistic approach to identifying, addressing, and recovering from cyber risks. This section introduces these functions and their relevance to SOC 2 compliance.

The following Table lists the NIST CSF 2.0 Core Function and Category names and unique alphabetic identifiers. Each Function name in the table is linked to its portion of the appendix. The order of Functions, Categories, and Subcategories of the Core is not alphabetical; it is intended to resonate most with those charged with operationalizing risk management within an organization.

Function	Category	Category Identifier
Govern (GV)	Organizational Context	GV.OC
	Risk Management Strategy	GV.RM
	Roles, Responsibilities, and Authorities	GV.RR
	Policy	GV.PO
	Oversight	GV.OV
	Cybersecurity Supply Chain Risk Management	GV.SC
Identify	Asset Management	ID.AM

(ID)	Risk Assessment	ID.RA
	Improvement	ID.IM
Protect (PR)	Identity Management, Authentication, and Access Control	PR.AA
	Awareness and Training	PR.AT
	Data Security	PR.DS
	Platform Security	PR.PS
	Technology Infrastructure Resilience	PR.IR
Detect (DE)	Continuous Monitoring	DE.CM
	Adverse Event Analysis	DE.AE
Respond (RS)	Incident Management	RS.MA
	Incident Analysis	RS.AN
	Incident Response Reporting and Communication	RS.CO
	Incident Mitigation	RS.MI
Recover (RC)	Incident Recovery Plan Execution	RC.RP

	Incident Recovery Communication	RC.CO

Table 1. National Institute of Standards and Technology (2024). NIST CSF 2.0 Core Function and Category Names and Identifiers

3.3: Conducting an Assessment with the Govern Function

The **Govern** function, newly introduced in CSF 2.0, emphasizes the need for a structured approach to cybersecurity governance and accountability. This function supports establishing policies, defining roles and responsibilities, and maintaining oversight over all cybersecurity activities.

1. **Establish Governance Policies**:
   - Review and document policies that govern cybersecurity practices, such as information security policies, data protection policies, and acceptable use policies.
   - **Assessment Action**: Check for policy gaps, outdated documentation, or areas where roles and responsibilities are unclear.
2. **Define Roles and Responsibilities**:

- Ensure that accountability for cybersecurity tasks, such as access management and incident response, is clearly assigned.
- **Assessment Action**: Verify that all roles related to security are documented and that each role has a designated individual or team.

3. **Risk Management Oversight**:
    - Evaluate your risk management processes to ensure they align with both CSF 2.0 and SOC 2 requirements.
    - **Assessment Action**: Confirm that risk assessments are performed regularly and documented, addressing both known and emerging threats.

3.4: Conducting an Assessment with the Identify Function

The **Identify** function focuses on asset management, risk assessment, and understanding critical business environments. This function is essential for establishing a clear inventory of assets and identifying potential cybersecurity risks.

1. **Inventory All Assets**:
    - Create a comprehensive inventory of all assets, including hardware, software, and

data, to ensure they are properly tracked and managed.
- **Assessment Action**: Confirm that each asset is documented and categorized based on its criticality and sensitivity to the organization.

2. **Conduct a Risk Assessment**:
   - Identify potential vulnerabilities and risks affecting each asset or system.
   - **Assessment Action**: Use risk assessment frameworks to evaluate the impact and likelihood of risks, and document findings for future action.
   - **Risk Transference:** An organization plan for risk transference example, is hiring a Cybersecurity Insurance, reducing costs over a breach or cyber event, covering:
     1. Remediation and Notification Expenses
     2. Crisis Management Expenses
     3. Data Loss
     4. Network Business Interruption Loss

3. **Prioritize Business Critical Functions**:
   - Understand which functions and processes are critical to your operations and require the highest level of protection.
   - **Assessment Action**: Identify and document key business processes and prioritize security measures for high-impact areas.

3.5: Conducting an Assessment with the Protect Function

The **Protect** function involves implementing controls and safeguards to protect systems and data from cybersecurity threats. This function aligns with SOC 2's **Security**, **Confidentiality**, and **Privacy** TSCs, and includes controls for access management, data security, and user training.

1. **Access Management**:
    - Evaluate current access controls, such as role-based access control (RBAC) and multi-factor authentication (MFA), to limit unauthorized access.
    - **Assessment Action**: Verify that access control policies are enforced, and that all privileged accounts are properly managed.
2. **Data Security and Encryption**:
    - Assess data protection measures, including encryption and data masking, to safeguard sensitive information.
    - **Assessment Action**: Check that sensitive data is encrypted at rest and in transit and that encryption standards meet industry benchmarks (e.g., AES-256).
3. **Employee Training and Security Awareness**:
    - Evaluate the effectiveness of your security awareness program to ensure employees

understand cybersecurity threats and best practices.
- **Assessment Action**: Review training records, simulate phishing tests, and measure employee compliance with security policies.

3.6: Conducting an Assessment with the Detect Function

The **Detect** function includes measures for continuous monitoring, anomaly detection, and incident identification, ensuring that potential security events are identified early. This function is essential to SOC 2 compliance, as it helps organizations respond to incidents proactively.

1. **Anomaly Detection**:
   - Implement systems to monitor for unusual activities or security events that may indicate a threat.
   - **Assessment Action**: Check for tools like SIEM (Security Information and Event Management) or IDS/IPS systems that can detect and alert on anomalies.
2. **Continuous Monitoring**:
   - Ensure continuous monitoring of critical systems to provide real-time alerts on potential security incidents.

- **Assessment Action**: Verify that monitoring is active and includes alerts for key security events (e.g., unauthorized access attempts).
3. **Log Management**:
    - Evaluate your logging and retention practices to ensure comprehensive event logging for security investigations.
    - **Assessment Action**: Review log configurations to confirm that logs are stored securely and are accessible for forensic purposes.

3.7: Conducting an Assessment with the Respond Function

The **Respond** function focuses on incident response, containment, and communication processes, allowing organizations to mitigate the impact of security incidents. Effective response plans are essential for maintaining SOC 2 compliance, as they help limit disruptions and restore services quickly.

1. **Incident Response Plan (IRP)**:
    - Review and test your organization's IRP to ensure it outlines clear steps for identifying, containing, and eradicating security incidents.

- **Assessment Action**: Verify that the IRP is documented, accessible, and regularly tested through simulations or tabletop exercises.
2. **Communication Protocols**:
    - Ensure that communication plans are in place to notify stakeholders and employees during and after an incident.
    - **Assessment Action**: Check that notification procedures are clear and include templates or guidelines for informing affected parties.
3. **Post-Incident Analysis**:
    - Conduct post-incident reviews to analyze causes and implement improvements.
    - **Assessment Action**: Verify that incident reports are documented, and lessons learned are integrated into updated security practices.

3.8: Conducting an Assessment with the Recover Function

The **Recover** function focuses on restoring systems and services after an incident, ensuring business continuity and data integrity. This function aligns with SOC 2's **Availability** and **Processing Integrity** TSCs, supporting the rapid restoration of operations.

1. **Develop and Test Recovery Plans**:
    - Ensure that recovery plans are in place, documented, and tested regularly to confirm

they are effective in restoring critical systems.
- **Assessment Action**: Review test results from disaster recovery (DR) and business continuity plan (BCP) exercises to ensure they meet recovery time objectives (RTOs).
2. **Data Restoration and Validation**:
    - Verify that data can be fully restored and validated for accuracy following an incident.
    - **Assessment Action**: Check that backup and restoration processes are functional and meet organizational requirements for data integrity.
3. **Coordinate Stakeholder Communication**:
    - Ensure a plan is in place to coordinate communications with stakeholders during the recovery process.
    - **Assessment Action**: Verify that recovery communications protocols are documented and tested for clarity and effectiveness.

3.9: Documenting the NIST CSF 2.0 Assessment Findings

This section guides readers on documenting the findings from their NIST CSF 2.0 assessment, providing a baseline for future improvements and a roadmap for meeting SOC 2 compliance requirements.

1. **Create a Gap Analysis Report**:
   - Summarize the assessment findings, highlighting areas where current controls do not meet NIST CSF or SOC 2 requirements.
   - **Assessment Action**: Prioritize identified gaps based on their impact and the effort needed to address them.
2. **Develop an Action Plan**:
   - Outline a structured plan to address assessment gaps and bring your security practices in line with NIST CSF and SOC 2 requirements.
   - **Assessment Action**: Assign responsibilities, set deadlines, and monitor progress to ensure timely remediation.
3. **Prepare Documentation for Audits**:
   - Organize findings, policies, and evidence into a format that can be easily referenced during a SOC 2 audit.
   - **Assessment Action**: Create a centralized repository for documents, organized by NIST CSF function and corresponding SOC 2 TSC.

Chapter 4

Mapping Our Company's NIST CSF Assessment to SOC 2 Trust Services Criteria (TSCs)

This chapter explores how to map your organization's **NIST Cybersecurity Framework (CSF) 2.0** assessment to the **SOC 2 Trust Services Criteria (TSC)**, aligning NIST's updated functions: **Govern, Identify, Protect, Detect, Respond, and Recover**, with the SOC 2 compliance requirements. Through this alignment, your organization can ensure a comprehensive approach to cybersecurity that meets SOC 2 standards while enhancing overall resilience. Each NIST CSF 2.0 function is reviewed with guidance on mapping controls to the relevant SOC 2 TSCs, providing an integrated approach to address cybersecurity requirements and compliance.

4.1: Overview of the NIST CSF and SOC 2 TSCs

4.1.1: NIST CSF and SOC 2 TSCs: An Integrated Approach

While NIST CSF is a flexible framework that focuses on managing cybersecurity risks, SOC 2 compliance specifically addresses how systems protect customer data. However, there is a significant overlap between the two, and by aligning the NIST CSF's core functions: Govern, Identify, Protect, Detect, Respond, and Recover, with SOC 2 TSCs, startups and SMBs can streamline the compliance process.

- **NIST CSF Core Functions**:
    1. **Govern**: Emphasizes the need for a structured approach to cybersecurity governance and accountability.
    2. **Identify**: Understanding assets, systems, and risks.
    3. **Protect**: Implementing safeguards to ensure service delivery.
    4. **Detect**: Detecting security events and anomalies.
    5. **Respond**: Responding to incidents effectively.
    6. **Recover**: Restoring operations post-incident.
- **SOC 2 Trust Services Criteria (TSC)**:
    1. **Security**: Protecting against unauthorized access (both physical and logical).

2. **Availability**: Ensuring system availability as per service agreements.
3. **Processing Integrity**: Ensuring systems process data accurately and reliably.
4. **Confidentiality**: Protecting confidential information.
5. **Privacy**: Handling personal information according to agreed-upon privacy policies.

Why Align NIST CSF with SOC 2? For startups and SMBs, mapping NIST CSF to SOC 2:

- Simplifies the compliance process by leveraging existing security practices.
- Reduces duplication of efforts, especially for businesses already following NIST CSF.
- Enhances the security posture while simultaneously working towards SOC 2 certification.

4.1.2: How NIST CSF Supports SOC 2 TSCs

Here's a high-level look at how each NIST CSF function corresponds to SOC 2 criteria:

NIST CSF Function	SOC 2 TSC	Example Controls
Govern	Security, Condifentiality, Privacy	Governance policies and procedures, risk management, compliance
Identify	Security, Availability, Confidentiality	Asset inventories, risk assessments, data classification
Protect	Security, Processing Integrity, Confidentiality	Access control, encryption, system hardening
Detect	Security, Processing Integrity	Logging, continuous monitoring, threat detection
Respond	Security, Availability	Incident response, communication plans, containment procedures
Recover	Availability, Processing Integrity	Backup and recovery, disaster recovery plans

Table 2. Mapping NIST CF Function to SOC 2

4.2: Mapping the Govern Function to SOC 2 TSCs

The new **Govern** function in NIST CSF 2.0 emphasizes organizational accountability, policies, and risk management, forming a strong foundation for all cybersecurity activities. SOC 2's **Security** and **Confidentiality** TSCs align closely with Govern's focus on establishing clear oversight and accountability in managing cybersecurity.

1. **Governance Structures and Policies**:
   - Develop cybersecurity governance policies that define roles, responsibilities, and accountability across the organization.
   - **Mapping to SOC 2**: SOC 2's Security TSC requires documented policies and a well-defined governance framework, aligning with the Govern function's focus on setting up structures for oversight and accountability.
2. **Risk Management and Compliance**:
   - Implement risk assessment and compliance monitoring practices that ensure adherence to cybersecurity policies and industry standards.
   - **Mapping to SOC 2**: The Common Criteria within SOC 2 emphasize risk assessment and

monitoring, which are integral parts of the Govern function.

4.3: Mapping the Identify Function to SOC 2 TSCs

The **Identify** function in NIST CSF 2.0 addresses the need to understand organizational assets, risks, and dependencies. This function supports SOC 2's **Security**, **Availability**, and **Confidentiality** TSCs by ensuring that critical assets are documented and protected against threats.

1. **Asset Management and Inventory**:
   - Create a comprehensive inventory of all hardware, software, data, and personnel that are critical to cybersecurity operations.
   - **Mapping to SOC 2**: SOC 2's Security TSC requires organizations to maintain a clear inventory of assets, aligning closely with Identify's asset management requirements.
2. **Risk and Vulnerability Assessment**:
   - Conduct risk assessments to identify potential vulnerabilities and prioritize mitigation efforts.
   - **Mapping to SOC 2**: SOC 2's Common Criteria require regular risk assessments to evaluate threats to critical assets, aligning with the Identify function's emphasis on risk and vulnerability management.

4.4: Mapping the Protect Function to SOC 2 TSCs

The **Protect** function focuses on implementing safeguards to secure assets, systems, and data from cybersecurity threats. This aligns with SOC 2's **Security**, **Confidentiality**, and **Privacy** TSCs, which emphasize the need for robust controls to prevent unauthorized access and data breaches.

1. **Access Control Measures**:
    - Enforce strict access control measures, such as multi-factor authentication (MFA) and role-based access control (RBAC), to protect sensitive systems and data.
    - **Mapping to SOC 2**: SOC 2's Security and Confidentiality TSCs require controls to prevent unauthorized access, directly aligning with Protect's access control requirements.
2. **Data Protection and Encryption**:
    - Protect data through encryption, both at rest and in transit, and implement controls to maintain data confidentiality.
    - **Mapping to SOC 2**: The Confidentiality and Privacy TSCs require data encryption for sensitive information, aligning with Protect's emphasis on safeguarding data integrity and privacy.

3. **Employee Security Awareness and Training**:
    - Develop a cybersecurity awareness program to ensure that employees understand and follow best practices.
    - **Mapping to SOC 2**: SOC 2's Security TSC includes training requirements, which align with Protect's focus on security awareness.

4.5: Mapping the Detect Function to SOC 2 TSCs

The **Detect** function includes capabilities for monitoring, logging, and detecting cybersecurity events in real-time. This function directly supports SOC 2's **Security** and **Availability** TSCs, ensuring that incidents are promptly identified and managed to minimize impact.

1. **Continuous Monitoring**:
    - Implement real-time monitoring systems to detect anomalies and potential security incidents.
    - **Mapping to SOC 2**: SOC 2's Security TSC requires monitoring for potential threats, which aligns with the Detect function's continuous monitoring category.
2. **Anomaly and Incident Detection**:
    - Use automated tools to detect unusual activities or configurations that could indicate a security breach.

- **Mapping to SOC 2**: SOC 2's Security and Availability TSCs require mechanisms for anomaly detection, aligning with Detect's proactive approach to identifying security threats.
3. **Log Management and Analysis**:
    - Centralize logging and analysis to support event detection and forensic investigation if an incident occurs.
    - **Mapping to SOC 2**: SOC 2's Security TSC emphasizes event logging and monitoring, directly aligning with Detect's focus on maintaining logs and conducting analysis.

4.6: Mapping the Respond Function to SOC 2 TSCs

The **Respond** function outlines processes for managing and containing security incidents, ensuring minimal impact on operations. This function supports SOC 2's **Security** and **Confidentiality** TSCs by providing a structured response to detected threats and incidents.

1. **Incident Response Plan (IRP)**:
    - Develop and regularly test an incident response plan that outlines steps for identifying, containing, and eradicating threats.

- **Mapping to SOC 2**: SOC 2's Security TSC requires an incident response plan to address and contain security events, aligning with Respond's emphasis on incident management.
2. **Communication and Coordination**:
    - Implement communication protocols to ensure stakeholders are informed of incidents and response activities.
    - **Mapping to SOC 2**: SOC 2's Confidentiality and Security TSCs benefit from Respond's focus on communication, ensuring transparency and accountability during incident response.
3. **Post-Incident Analysis and Reporting**:
    - Conduct a post-incident review to analyze root causes, document lessons learned, and improve future response efforts.
    - **Mapping to SOC 2**: SOC 2's Common Criteria encourage continuous improvement, aligning with Respond's post-incident analysis for better incident response.

4.7: Mapping the Recover Function to SOC 2 TSCs

The **Recover** function addresses the importance of restoring normal operations after an incident, with a focus on resilience and continuity. This function aligns closely with

SOC 2's **Availability** and **Processing Integrity** TSCs, which require organizations to ensure that systems can be restored to reliable and accurate states after a disruption.

1. **Recovery Planning and Testing**:
   - Develop, document, and test recovery plans to restore critical systems following an incident.
   - **Mapping to SOC 2**: SOC 2's Availability TSC requires recovery procedures, aligning with Recover's focus on ensuring resilience and continuity of operations.
2. **System Restoration and Data Integrity**:
   - Implement processes to restore data integrity and validate system functionality after recovery.
   - **Mapping to SOC 2**: The Processing Integrity TSC aligns with Recover's emphasis on maintaining data accuracy and restoring system functions post-incident.
3. **Stakeholder Communication and Coordination**:
   - Define communication protocols for coordinating recovery activities with stakeholders and informing them of status updates.
   - **Mapping to SOC 2**: SOC 2's Availability TSC values clear communication during system recovery, aligning with Recover's

requirement for effective stakeholder coordination.

4.8: Practical Steps for Mapping NIST CSF 2.0 to SOC 2 TSCs

This section outlines a step-by-step approach to mapping NIST CSF 2.0 controls to SOC 2 TSCs, offering practical guidance on managing overlapping requirements efficiently.

1. **Cross-Reference NIST CSF and SOC 2 Controls**:
   - Develop a mapping document that identifies where each NIST CSF 2.0 control aligns with SOC 2 TSCs to streamline compliance efforts.
   - **Example**: Mapping NIST CSF's Protect function to SOC 2's Security and Confidentiality TSCs for unified access control implementation.
2. **Document Control Alignment for Audits**:
   - Record how each NIST CSF 2.0 control fulfills SOC 2 requirements, ensuring documentation is available for auditors.
   - **Example**: Document how continuous monitoring tools address both Detect function requirements and SOC 2's Availability TSC.
3. **Identify and Address Gaps**:

- Review any gaps identified in the mapping and take corrective actions to implement controls that meet both NIST CSF 2.0 and SOC 2 criteria.
- **Example**: If anomaly detection tools are missing, prioritize acquiring a solution that satisfies both frameworks.

Chapter 5

Creating a NIST CSF Current Profile for Our Company

In this chapter, we focus on developing a **Current Profile** using the NIST Cybersecurity Framework (CSF). The Current Profile provides a clear picture of your company's existing cybersecurity practices, allowing you to assess the effectiveness of your current controls, processes, and technologies. For startups and SMBs, the Current Profile is essential for understanding where your organization stands in terms of risk management and identifying areas for improvement. This chapter will guide you step-by-step on how to create a NIST CSF Current Profile and use it as a foundation for building a stronger cybersecurity program.

5.1: Purpose and Benefits of a Current Profile

5.1.1: Understanding the Current Profile

A **Current Profile** is an assessment of your organization's existing cybersecurity controls and practices, structured around the NIST CSF 2.0 functions. This profile helps identify gaps and areas for improvement, providing a clear view of your security posture as it stands today.

5.1.2: How the Current Profile Supports SOC 2 Compliance

Creating a Current Profile aligned with NIST CSF 2.0 also supports SOC 2 Trust Services Criteria (TSC) compliance by revealing how existing controls meet security, availability, confidentiality, and privacy requirements. This alignment allows for an efficient compliance roadmap and a structured approach to meeting audit expectations.

5.2: Assessing the Govern Function for the Current Profile

The **Govern** function emphasizes organizational accountability, cybersecurity policies, and governance processes. Assessing this function helps ensure that clear policies and accountability structures are in place.

1. **Review Governance Policies and Documentation**:

- Identify all existing cybersecurity policies, including information security, data governance, and risk management policies.
- **Current Profile Action**: Evaluate the completeness, relevance, and currency of each policy.

2. **Evaluate Accountability and Oversight Structures**:
   - Review how cybersecurity responsibilities are assigned and overseen within the organization.
   - **Current Profile Action**: Confirm that key roles, responsibilities, and reporting lines are clearly documented and communicated.

3. **Compliance and Risk Management**:
   - Assess existing processes for managing regulatory compliance and risk.
   - **Current Profile Action**: Verify that the organization has a formal risk management process and a process for monitoring compliance with industry standards and regulations.

5.3: Assessing the Identify Function for the Current Profile

The **Identify** function focuses on gaining a clear understanding of assets, risks, and vulnerabilities across the organization. This function helps ensure that all critical resources and potential cybersecurity risks are documented.

1. **Asset Inventory**:
   - Review and update the organization's inventory of all hardware, software, data, and critical personnel.
   - **Current Profile Action**: Confirm that all critical assets are cataloged and assigned an owner responsible for managing security.
2. **Risk Assessment**:
   - Identify and document the current processes for conducting risk assessments, including methods for evaluating threats and vulnerabilities.
   - **Current Profile Action**: Review recent risk assessments to understand current and emerging threats to the organization.
3. **Data Classification**:
   - Examine data classification practices to ensure that all data is categorized based on sensitivity and criticality.
   - **Current Profile Action**: Validate that sensitive data is identified, labeled, and

adequately protected based on its classification level.

5.4: Assessing the Protect Function for the Current Profile

The **Protect** function involves safeguards that prevent unauthorized access to data and systems. This function is critical for ensuring the organization's ability to protect information assets and meet SOC 2's Security and Confidentiality TSCs.

1. **Access Control Mechanisms**:
   - Assess the existing access control systems, such as role-based access control (RBAC) and multi-factor authentication (MFA), to prevent unauthorized access.
   - **Current Profile Action**: Ensure access is granted based on role requirements, with periodic reviews to remove outdated access.
2. **Data Protection Measures**:
   - Review controls for data encryption, both at rest and in transit, and evaluate data masking and tokenization practices where applicable.
   - **Current Profile Action**: Verify that sensitive data is encrypted according to industry standards and that controls are documented.

3. **Security Awareness and Training**:
    - Assess current employee training and awareness programs focused on cybersecurity.
    - **Current Profile Action**: Document training completion rates and confirm that staff are educated on core security policies and risks.

5.5: Assessing the Detect Function for the Current Profile

The **Detect** function includes measures for continuous monitoring and anomaly detection to identify cybersecurity events quickly. This function is crucial for enabling rapid incident detection and response.

1. **Continuous Monitoring**:
    - Review the systems in place for real-time monitoring of networks and systems for potential threats.
    - **Current Profile Action**: Confirm that monitoring tools (e.g., SIEM, IDS/IPS) are configured to provide alerts for suspicious activities.
2. **Anomaly Detection**:
    - Evaluate current practices for detecting unusual behavior or system anomalies that may indicate a cybersecurity incident.

- **Current Profile Action**: Ensure that anomaly detection tools are in place and that alerts are configured to notify relevant personnel.

3. **Logging and Log Management**:
    - Assess logging capabilities, including which events are logged and how long logs are retained for analysis and compliance.
    - **Current Profile Action**: Confirm that logs are stored securely and can be retrieved for forensic investigation when needed.

5.6: Assessing the Respond Function for the Current Profile

The **Respond** function focuses on incident response and containment to minimize the impact of detected cybersecurity incidents. This function is essential for meeting SOC 2's Security and Confidentiality TSCs by demonstrating your organization's readiness to manage security events.

1. **Incident Response Plan**:
    - Review the organization's incident response plan (IRP) and determine if it provides clear steps for detection, containment, and eradication of threats.

- **Current Profile Action**: Document whether the IRP is tested periodically and updated to address new threat scenarios.
2. **Communication Protocols**:
    - Evaluate existing communication protocols for notifying stakeholders and coordinating response efforts during incidents.
    - **Current Profile Action**: Confirm that incident notifications are timely, documented, and include key stakeholders.
3. **Post-Incident Review**:
    - Assess whether a post-incident analysis is conducted for all incidents to identify root causes and implement improvements.
    - **Current Profile Action**: Review incident reports for trends and verify that lessons learned are documented and integrated into future security practices.

5.7: Assessing the Recover Function for the Current Profile

The **Recover** function focuses on restoring systems and operations after an incident, with an emphasis on resilience and continuity. This function supports SOC 2's Availability and Processing Integrity TSCs by ensuring that the organization can quickly recover from disruptions.

1. **Recovery Planning and Testing**:
   - Review disaster recovery (DR) and business continuity planning (BCP) documentation to ensure that recovery strategies are in place and tested.
   - **Current Profile Action**: Validate that DR and BCP exercises are performed regularly and meet recovery time objectives (RTOs) for critical systems.
2. **Data Restoration and Validation**:
   - Assess processes for data backup, restoration, and validation to ensure that data integrity can be preserved after an incident.
   - **Current Profile Action**: Confirm that backups are regularly tested and that restoration processes meet organizational requirements for accuracy and timeliness.
3. **Communication During Recovery**:
   - Evaluate the organization's communication strategy for notifying stakeholders and coordinating efforts during the recovery process.
   - **Current Profile Action**: Ensure that communication protocols are well-documented and tested for effectiveness during recovery.

5.8: Documenting the Current Profile and Preparing for Future Improvements

After completing assessments across all six functions of NIST CSF 2.0, it's essential to document the findings, which form your organization's Current Profile. This documentation serves as a baseline for future improvement and compliance initiatives.

1. **Compile a Gap Analysis Report**:
   - Summarize gaps identified in each function, highlighting areas that require immediate attention for SOC 2 compliance.
   - **Current Profile Action**: Prioritize remediation efforts based on risk levels and compliance needs.
2. **Create an Action Plan for Improvement**:
   - Develop an action plan outlining steps to address the identified gaps, assign responsibilities, and establish timelines.
   - **Current Profile Action**: Use this plan as a roadmap for progressing from the Current Profile to the Target Profile.
3. **Prepare Documentation for Auditors**:
   - Organize the Current Profile documentation for easy access during audits, ensuring alignment with both NIST CSF 2.0 and SOC 2 criteria.

- **Current Profile Action**: Centralize documentation in a secure repository to facilitate future audit processes and compliance tracking.

Chapter 6

Creating a NIST CSF 2.0 Target Profile for Our Company

This chapter guides you through developing a **Target Profile** based on the **NIST Cybersecurity Framework (CSF) 2.0**. A Target Profile represents the desired state of your organization's cybersecurity capabilities across the six NIST CSF core functions: **Govern, Identify, Protect, Detect, Respond, and Recover**. By defining a Target Profile, your organization can set clear, actionable goals for enhancing its cybersecurity posture and meeting **SOC 2 Trust Services Criteria (TSC)** requirements. Each function is examined to provide a roadmap for achieving a robust security environment that aligns with regulatory compliance, industry best practices, and organizational goals.

6.1: Purpose and Benefits of a Target Profile

6.1.1: Understanding the Target Profile

A **Target Profile** outlines the ideal security controls, processes, and practices that your organization aims to implement. It is structured around the NIST CSF 2.0 functions and serves as a benchmark for building a resilient cybersecurity program.

6.1.2: How the Target Profile Supports SOC 2 Compliance

By aligning the Target Profile with SOC 2 Trust Services Criteria, your organization can prioritize and implement controls that meet SOC 2 standards for **Security**, **Availability**, **Confidentiality**, and **Privacy**. The Target Profile provides a structured roadmap for addressing compliance requirements and enhancing overall cybersecurity resilience.

6.2: Defining the Target Profile for the Govern Function

The **Govern** function focuses on establishing organizational oversight, accountability, and risk management for cybersecurity. In the Target Profile, this function sets the groundwork for consistent security governance practices.

1. **Establish Comprehensive Governance Policies**:
   o Define, document, and enforce cybersecurity policies across the organization, covering areas such as risk management, compliance, and information security.
   o **Target Profile Action**: Set a goal to have a formal governance policy reviewed and updated annually to reflect evolving risks and regulations.
2. **Strengthen Accountability and Oversight**:
   o Create accountability structures that ensure clear roles, responsibilities, and regular reporting for all cybersecurity functions.
   o **Target Profile Action**: Implement regular oversight by senior management, ensuring that cybersecurity is prioritized as part of strategic decision-making.
3. **Develop a Risk Management Strategy**:
   o Define a risk management process to identify, assess, and prioritize security risks regularly.
   o **Target Profile Action**: Set up quarterly risk assessments to ensure that risk management remains current and addresses both internal and external threats.

6.3: Defining the Target Profile for the Identify Function

The **Identify** function in the Target Profile emphasizes a comprehensive understanding of assets, risks, and resources. This foundation ensures your organization can proactively manage and protect critical assets.

1. **Create a Detailed Asset Inventory**:
    - Develop a systematic approach to cataloging and managing assets, including hardware, software, data, and personnel critical to cybersecurity.
    - **Target Profile Action**: Ensure the asset inventory is updated in real time, with assigned owners responsible for each asset's security.
2. **Implement Enhanced Risk Assessment Processes**:
    - Design and formalize risk assessment procedures to evaluate vulnerabilities and prioritize risk mitigation actions.
    - **Target Profile Action**: Plan to conduct bi-annual risk assessments, using a risk-ranking system to prioritize mitigation efforts for high-impact assets.
3. **Implement Data Classification and Labeling**:
    - Establish a data classification policy to categorize information based on sensitivity

and implement corresponding security controls.
- **Target Profile Action**: Ensure data is labeled according to its classification and protected with access controls that reflect its sensitivity.

6.4: Defining the Target Profile for the Protect Function

The **Protect** function in the Target Profile involves proactive safeguards to secure systems, data, and networks against potential threats. This function includes essential controls for access management, data security, and employee awareness.

1. **Strengthen Access Control Systems**:
   - Implement advanced access control mechanisms, such as multi-factor authentication (MFA) and role-based access control (RBAC), to minimize unauthorized access.
   - **Target Profile Action**: Set a goal to enforce MFA across all administrative and high-privilege accounts within the next quarter.
2. **Enhance Data Protection and Encryption Standards**:

- Develop standards for data encryption at rest and in transit, ensuring that sensitive information is adequately safeguarded.
- **Target Profile Action**: Adopt a minimum encryption standard of AES-256 for sensitive data and plan to implement it across critical systems.

3. **Expand Security Awareness and Training Programs**:
    - Develop a comprehensive training program to increase employee understanding of security risks and best practices.
    - **Target Profile Action**: Plan quarterly security awareness training sessions and annual phishing simulations to reinforce good cyber hygiene.

6.5: Defining the Target Profile for the Detect Function

The **Detect** function in the Target Profile focuses on real-time monitoring, logging, and alerting capabilities to promptly identify cybersecurity incidents. Effective detection capabilities support rapid response and help minimize the impact of security events.

1. **Implement Advanced Threat Detection Tools**:

- Invest in tools that detect anomalies and potential threats in real time, such as Security Information and Event Management (SIEM) systems.
- **Target Profile Action**: Set up a centralized SIEM to aggregate logs from all critical systems, with real-time alerting configured for key security events.

2. **Establish Continuous Monitoring Protocols**:
   - Deploy continuous monitoring solutions that provide visibility into network and system activities.
   - **Target Profile Action**: Develop monitoring dashboards and configure alerts for high-risk anomalies, ensuring prompt identification of unusual activities.

3. **Strengthen Log Management and Retention Policies**:
   - Implement centralized log management practices to ensure that all critical events are recorded and accessible for analysis.
   - **Target Profile Action**: Define a policy to retain security logs for at least one year, with automated backups for forensic investigation if needed.

6.6: Defining the Target Profile for the Respond Function

The **Respond** function in the Target Profile includes robust incident response plans, containment strategies, and communication protocols, enabling your organization to minimize incident impact and resume normal operations quickly.

1. **Develop a Comprehensive Incident Response Plan (IRP)**:
    - Design an incident response plan that clearly outlines steps for identifying, containing, and mitigating security incidents.
    - **Target Profile Action**: Ensure the IRP includes defined escalation protocols and is tested through regular simulations or tabletop exercises.
2. **Implement Incident Communication and Coordination**:
    - Establish protocols for timely communication during incidents, ensuring that stakeholders are informed and coordinated.
    - **Target Profile Action**: Define roles for incident communication, ensuring that team members and stakeholders are updated based on incident severity.
3. **Enhance Post-Incident Analysis Processes**:

- Implement processes for conducting root-cause analysis and post-incident reviews to strengthen future response capabilities.
- **Target Profile Action**: Require a documented review for every incident, with lessons learned and recommendations integrated into the IRP.

6.7: Defining the Target Profile for the Recover Function

The **Recover** function focuses on building resilience by ensuring systems, services, and data can be restored after an incident. A robust Recover function supports SOC 2's Availability and Processing Integrity TSCs, ensuring reliable recovery from disruptions.

1. **Establish and Regularly Test Recovery Plans**:
   - Develop disaster recovery (DR) and business continuity (BC) plans that cover critical systems and business processes.
   - **Target Profile Action**: Test DR and BC plans bi-annually to confirm recovery time objectives (RTOs) are achievable and that staff understand recovery procedures.
2. **Ensure Data Backup and Integrity**:

- Implement data backup policies that support secure, regular backups of critical systems and data.
- **Target Profile Action**: Schedule daily backups for critical data and test recovery procedures quarterly to verify data integrity and accessibility.

3. **Formalize Communication During Recovery**:
   - Create clear communication plans for coordinating recovery activities and informing stakeholders post-incident.
   - **Target Profile Action**: Define communication protocols for recovery scenarios, including regular updates to key stakeholders and customers as needed.

6.8: Documenting the Target Profile and Setting Goals for Future Improvements

After defining the Target Profile across all six functions, the next step is to document the goals and desired security outcomes. This documentation acts as a roadmap for achieving the Target Profile and closing gaps identified in the Current Profile.

1. **Create a Gap Analysis and Action Plan**:
    - Perform a gap analysis comparing the Current and Target Profiles, identifying specific areas for improvement.
    - **Target Profile Action**: Prioritize gap-closing actions based on their impact on SOC 2 compliance and overall risk reduction.
2. **Establish Milestones and Deadlines**:
    - Set clear milestones for implementing each element of the Target Profile, ensuring that security goals are achievable within a defined timeframe.
    - **Target Profile Action**: Assign deadlines and responsible teams to each control or process that needs enhancement to meet the Target Profile standards.
3. **Prepare for SOC 2 Audits and Continuous Improvement**:
    - Use the Target Profile documentation to support SOC 2 audit readiness and to facilitate continuous cybersecurity improvement.

Target Profile Action: Document each improvement and control implementation to ensure an organized and proactive approach to compliance and security.

Chapter 7

Assessing NIST CSF 2.0 Tiers for Use in Current and Target Profiles

In this chapter, we explore how to use the **NIST CSF 2.0 Implementation Tiers** to evaluate and guide your organization's cybersecurity maturity level. The Tiers: **Partial, Risk Informed, Repeatable,** and **Adaptive**, represent a spectrum of cybersecurity maturity, from basic risk management practices to advanced, adaptive cybersecurity strategies. By assessing your organization's current Tier level and setting a target Tier, you can prioritize improvements and align your cybersecurity practices with both **SOC 2 compliance** requirements and business objectives. Each Tier is explored with examples of practices, controls, and governance structures to help organizations establish realistic and strategic goals.

.

7.1: Understanding the Purpose and Benefits of NIST CSF 2.0 Tiers

7.1.1: Overview of the Implementation Tiers

NIST CSF 2.0 introduces four Implementation Tiers, each reflecting a different level of cybersecurity maturity and risk management capability. These Tiers help organizations understand where they are in terms of cybersecurity practices and provide guidance on how to advance to a higher level if desired.

- **Partial (Tier 1)**: Limited or ad hoc cybersecurity practices.
- **Risk Informed (Tier 2)**: Risk management practices are developed but not consistently applied.
- **Repeatable (Tier 3)**: Established risk management processes that are regularly updated.
- **Adaptive (Tier 4)**: Advanced, adaptive practices that respond dynamically to changing threats.

7.1.2: How Implementation Tiers Support SOC 2 Compliance

Using the Implementation Tiers helps align your organization's cybersecurity posture with **SOC 2 Trust Services Criteria (TSC)**. By setting a target Tier, you create a roadmap for improving your cybersecurity maturity, implementing controls, and demonstrating a structured approach to risk management, which is critical for SOC 2 compliance.

7.2: Tier 1 – Partial

Partial (Tier 1) is the most basic level, where cybersecurity practices are ad hoc and risk management processes are limited or informal. Organizations at this Tier may have minimal resources dedicated to cybersecurity, and their practices are often reactive.

1. **Characteristics of Tier 1**:
    - Limited risk awareness and inconsistent cybersecurity practices across the organization.
    - No formal governance structures for cybersecurity, and security responsibilities are often unclear.
2. **Examples of Controls and Practices**:
    - **Basic Asset Management**: A simple inventory of critical systems may exist, but it is not consistently updated.
    - **Minimal Access Control**: Basic controls may be in place for high-risk areas but are not enforced uniformly.

- **Reactive Incident Response**: Incidents are handled on a case-by-case basis without a formal incident response plan.
3. **SOC 2 Compliance Considerations**:
   - Organizations at Tier 1 will need to develop and formalize processes to meet SOC 2 requirements for consistent security practices, documented policies, and clear roles.

7.3: Tier 2 – Risk Informed

Risk Informed (Tier 2) represents a level where the organization has started to develop and implement cybersecurity practices based on identified risks, though these practices may still be inconsistently applied across the organization.

1. **Characteristics of Tier 2**:
   - Risk assessments are conducted, but the results may not be systematically applied to all parts of the organization.
   - Governance structures begin to emerge, with assigned responsibilities for cybersecurity, though processes may lack maturity.
2. **Examples of Controls and Practices**:
   - **Documented Policies**: Initial policies for access control, data protection, and incident

response are established but may lack regular updates.
- **Basic Monitoring**: Some level of monitoring for security events is implemented, though it may not be comprehensive.
- **Defined Risk Assessments**: Formal risk assessments are conducted periodically, but responses to findings may be inconsistent.
3. **SOC 2 Compliance Considerations**:
    - Moving from Tier 1 to Tier 2 often involves establishing consistent documentation, updating policies, and improving awareness of risks, which are fundamental steps toward SOC 2 readiness.

7.4: Tier 3 – Repeatable

Repeatable (Tier 3) represents an organization with defined and consistently applied cybersecurity practices that are regularly reviewed and updated. Risk management is integrated into broader business practices, and governance structures are well established.

1. **Characteristics of Tier 3**:
    - Formalized and standardized cybersecurity policies and procedures, with accountability across departments.

- Regular risk assessments and monitoring practices are in place, and the organization responds proactively to identified risks.

2. **Examples of Controls and Practices**:
    - **Formal Incident Response Plan (IRP)**: A documented IRP is in place, with regular testing through simulations or tabletop exercises.
    - **Comprehensive Access Management**: Access is managed with role-based access control (RBAC) and multi-factor authentication (MFA) for high-privilege accounts.
    - **Automated Monitoring and Alerts**: Security Information and Event Management (SIEM) systems and automated alerts help detect and respond to anomalies.

3. **SOC 2 Compliance Considerations**:
    - Tier 3 aligns well with SOC 2 requirements, as it demonstrates consistent, well-documented controls. Organizations at this Tier are typically well-prepared for SOC 2 audits, with clear policies and regular evidence of control effectiveness.

7.5: Tier 4 – Adaptive

Adaptive (Tier 4) represents the highest level of cybersecurity maturity, where the organization uses advanced tools and adaptive strategies to respond dynamically to changing threats and cybersecurity risks. Practices are continuously improved and are highly integrated with organizational objectives.

1. **Characteristics of Tier 4**:
   - Cybersecurity practices are highly proactive, and the organization is agile in responding to evolving threats.
   - Threat intelligence and incident response are highly sophisticated, and the organization uses data analytics and machine learning to anticipate and adapt to risks.
2. **Examples of Controls and Practices**:
   - **Proactive Threat Intelligence**: Using threat intelligence feeds and predictive analytics to anticipate and respond to emerging threats.
   - **Advanced Incident Response Automation**: Automated incident response workflows allow for rapid containment and mitigation of security events.
   - **Continuous Improvement Processes**: Cybersecurity practices are continuously evaluated and optimized based on feedback,

threat intelligence, and incident post-mortems.
3. **SOC 2 Compliance Considerations**:
    o Tier 4 practices far exceed SOC 2 requirements and demonstrate advanced cybersecurity capabilities. Organizations at this Tier are positioned as leaders in cybersecurity and may leverage their high maturity to meet the most stringent client and regulatory requirements.

7.6: Selecting a Target Tier for Your Organization

The Target Tier you select should reflect your organization's size, risk tolerance, industry requirements, and available resources. For most startups and SMBs, achieving **Tier 2 (Risk Informed)** or **Tier 3 (Repeatable)** provides a solid cybersecurity foundation and aligns well with SOC 2 requirements.

1. **Factors to Consider**:
    o **Regulatory Requirements**: Industry regulations may require a specific Tier for compliance.
    o **Business Objectives**: Select a Tier that aligns with the strategic goals of your organization and the level of risk you are willing to manage.

- **Resource Availability**: Consider available budget, staff expertise, and technology resources, as advancing Tiers often requires more sophisticated tools and trained personnel.

2. **Defining Tier Advancement Goals**:
   - If your Current Profile is at Tier 1 or Tier 2, set goals for progressing to the next Tier. Define specific actions, such as developing policies, automating monitoring, or formalizing incident response.

7.7: Documenting the Current and Target Tier Assessments

Documenting both your Current Tier and Target Tier helps establish a roadmap for cybersecurity improvement. This documentation can be used to justify investments in cybersecurity and to communicate progress to stakeholders.

1. **Create a Tier Assessment Report**:
   - Document your organization's Current Tier, the selected Target Tier, and the gap between the two. Summarize your findings, and outline action steps to close identified gaps.
2. **Set Milestones and Metrics**:
   - Define specific milestones and metrics for advancing through the Tiers. Regularly

measure progress to ensure continuous improvement and alignment with the Target Profile.

3. **Align Tier Goals with SOC 2 Compliance**:
    - Ensure that the Tier advancement goals are directly aligned with SOC 2 Trust Services Criteria, providing a structured path toward compliance.

Chapter 8

Analyzing the Gaps Between our NIST CSF 2.0 Current and Target Profiles

In this chapter, we focus on identifying and analyzing the gaps between your organization's **Current Profile** and **Target Profile** based on the **NIST Cybersecurity Framework (CSF) 2.0**. This gap analysis highlights areas where improvements are needed across the six NIST CSF core functions: **Govern, Identify, Protect, Detect, Respond, and Recover**, to reach your desired cybersecurity posture. By addressing these gaps, your organization can better align with **SOC 2 Trust Services Criteria (TSC)** and strengthen its overall security framework. Each function is examined to provide clear guidance on assessing, prioritizing, and closing gaps for optimal security and compliance readiness.

8.1: Purpose and Benefits of a Gap Analysis

8.1.1: Understanding the Role of Gap Analysis

A **gap analysis** compares your organization's Current Profile with its Target Profile, identifying specific areas where improvements are needed. This process helps clarify the steps required to move from your current cybersecurity state to your desired state.

8.1.2: How Gap Analysis Supports SOC 2 Compliance

By mapping gaps across the NIST CSF 2.0 functions, your organization gains a clear roadmap for implementing controls that align with SOC 2 requirements. This analysis enables focused investments in cybersecurity measures that not only meet compliance but also enhance resilience against evolving threats.

8.2: Analyzing Gaps in the Govern Function

The **Govern** function addresses organizational structures, policies, and oversight mechanisms critical to effective cybersecurity management. Analyzing gaps in this function highlights areas where governance and accountability can be strengthened.

1. **Policy and Documentation Gaps**:
   - Identify missing or outdated policies related to risk management, information security, and data governance.
   - **Gap Analysis Action**: Document required policies and establish a review schedule to ensure they stay up-to-date with current standards and threats.
2. **Accountability and Oversight**:
   - Determine if cybersecurity roles and responsibilities are well-defined and whether oversight mechanisms are in place.
   - **Gap Analysis Action**: Assign ownership of key functions and ensure reporting lines are clear to support effective cybersecurity governance.
3. **Risk Management Integration**:
   - Assess if risk management practices are fully integrated into the organization's strategy and decision-making processes.
   - **Gap Analysis Action**: Develop a risk management process that includes regular assessments and board-level reporting on risk-related findings.

8.3: Analyzing Gaps in the Identify Function

The **Identify** function involves cataloging critical assets, managing risks, and establishing awareness of organizational resources. Analyzing gaps in this area helps ensure that all key assets and risks are documented and addressed.

1. **Asset Inventory and Ownership**:
    - Identify gaps in asset inventories, such as missing information on software, hardware, or data assets.
    - **Gap Analysis Action**: Ensure each critical asset is documented in a central repository with assigned ownership for ongoing management.
2. **Risk Assessment and Prioritization**:
    - Determine if risk assessments are conducted regularly and address all critical assets and vulnerabilities.
    - **Gap Analysis Action**: Schedule periodic risk assessments and document findings to prioritize risk mitigation efforts based on impact.
3. **Data Classification and Protection Needs**:
    - Check for gaps in data classification practices, especially for sensitive or regulated data.

- **Gap Analysis Action**: Implement a data classification framework to categorize information based on sensitivity and establish corresponding access controls.

8.4: Analyzing Gaps in the Protect Function

The **Protect** function includes safeguards to prevent unauthorized access and data breaches. Analyzing gaps here ensures that protection measures are comprehensive and aligned with SOC 2's Security, Confidentiality, and Privacy requirements.

1. **Access Control Deficiencies**:
    - Identify weaknesses in access control mechanisms, such as inconsistent enforcement of role-based access or lack of multi-factor authentication (MFA).
    - **Gap Analysis Action**: Implement standardized access control policies, enforce MFA for critical systems, and conduct regular access reviews.
2. **Data Encryption and Protection**:
    - Check if data protection measures, including encryption and backup procedures, are applied uniformly across sensitive information.

- **Gap Analysis Action**: Establish minimum encryption standards (e.g., AES-256) for data at rest and in transit, and verify that backup processes are tested regularly.
3. **Employee Training and Awareness**:
    - Assess the effectiveness and frequency of cybersecurity awareness programs for employees.
    - **Gap Analysis Action**: Create or update security training programs, including phishing simulations, to improve employee awareness and adherence to security policies.

8.5: Analyzing Gaps in the Detect Function

The **Detect** function focuses on identifying and monitoring security events in real time. Gaps in this function may limit your organization's ability to detect and respond to threats promptly, impacting compliance with SOC 2.

1. **Real-Time Monitoring Capabilities**:
    - Identify any missing tools or processes for continuous monitoring, such as SIEM systems or intrusion detection systems (IDS).
    - **Gap Analysis Action**: Implement or upgrade monitoring tools to enable real-time alerting and detection of suspicious activities.

2. **Anomaly Detection**:
    - Determine if existing systems can detect unusual patterns or potential threats across critical systems.
    - **Gap Analysis Action**: Configure anomaly detection tools to flag irregular behavior and send alerts for investigation by the security team.
3. **Log Management and Retention**:
    - Check for gaps in log management practices, such as insufficient log retention periods or lack of centralized log storage.
    - **Gap Analysis Action**: Standardize logging practices and configure logs to be stored securely with a retention policy that meets regulatory requirements.

8.6: Analyzing Gaps in the Respond Function

The **Respond** function includes incident response, containment, and communication processes essential to handling security incidents effectively. Gaps in this function affect your ability to mitigate and manage the impact of incidents.

1. **Incident Response Plan (IRP) Gaps**:

- Assess the incident response plan to identify missing elements, such as steps for containment, eradication, and recovery.
- **Gap Analysis Action**: Update the IRP to ensure it provides a comprehensive approach to handling security events, and conduct regular tests to validate its effectiveness.

2. **Communication Protocols During Incidents**:
    - Identify gaps in communication plans, such as unclear reporting structures or lack of contact lists for key stakeholders.
    - **Gap Analysis Action**: Define clear communication protocols for incidents, including stakeholder notification templates and escalation procedures.

3. **Post-Incident Analysis and Continuous Improvement**:
    - Check if there are procedures for post-incident analysis to identify root causes and prevent recurrence.
    - **Gap Analysis Action**: Implement post-incident reviews as a standard practice, documenting findings and integrating lessons learned into the response plan.

8.7: Analyzing Gaps in the Recover Function

The **Recover** function ensures that systems and data can be restored after an incident, supporting business continuity and resilience. Identifying gaps here is essential for fulfilling SOC 2's Availability and Processing Integrity criteria.

1. **Disaster Recovery (DR) and Business Continuity Plans (BCP)**:
    - Determine if DR and BCP documentation is comprehensive and if plans are regularly tested and updated.
    - **Gap Analysis Action**: Conduct semi-annual tests of DR and BCP procedures, with results documented and adjustments made based on testing outcomes.
2. **Data Backup and Restoration**:
    - Assess the organization's data backup and recovery processes to ensure that data can be restored accurately and in a timely manner.
    - **Gap Analysis Action**: Verify that backup schedules meet recovery objectives, and test restoration processes quarterly to confirm data integrity.
3. **Stakeholder Communication During Recovery**:
    - Identify any gaps in communication plans for the recovery phase, ensuring that stakeholders receive timely updates.

- **Gap Analysis Action**: Establish clear guidelines for communicating recovery progress and timelines with internal and external stakeholders.

8.8: Prioritizing and Documenting the Gap Analysis Findings

After identifying gaps across each NIST CSF 2.0 function, the next step is to prioritize these findings and document the actions needed to close the gaps. This will form the foundation of your organization's cybersecurity improvement plan.

1. **Develop a Prioritized Action Plan**:
   - Prioritize gaps based on risk impact, resource availability, and alignment with SOC 2 compliance requirements.
   - **Gap Analysis Action**: Assign responsibility for each gap-closing action and set achievable deadlines based on organizational priorities.
2. **Document Findings and Set Milestones**:
   - Create a gap analysis report that summarizes findings and defines milestones for achieving the Target Profile.
   - **Gap Analysis Action**: Use this document to track progress and ensure continuous

alignment with both NIST CSF 2.0 and SOC 2.

3. **Align Gap-Closing Activities with SOC 2 Compliance Goals**:
   - Map each action item to the corresponding SOC 2 TSC to ensure that your improvement plan is aligned with compliance goals.

Gap Analysis Action: Regularly review progress against compliance requirements, adjusting the plan as necessary to meet audit readiness.

Chapter 9

Understanding Why Configuration Management is the Center of the Universe

In this chapter, we focus on **configuration management (CM)** and explain why it plays a central role in cybersecurity. For startups and SMBs, configuration management serves as the backbone of a secure IT environment by ensuring that systems are consistently set up, maintained, and controlled. Configuration management affects every part of your cybersecurity framework, from asset management to incident response. This chapter will guide you through the importance of CM, how to create an effective configuration management strategy, and how CM connects to other essential security practices like asset management (AM), patch management (PM), and risk management (RM).

9.1: Where Everything Unveils – The Importance of Configuration Management

9.1.1: What is Configuration Management?

Configuration Management (CM) is the process of systematically managing and maintaining the settings, software, hardware, and configurations of an organization's IT environment. It ensures that all systems are properly configured, updated, and controlled throughout their lifecycle. This includes cloud and on-premises servers, databases, applications, network devices, and endpoints. CM involves from assets and resources authorization, to tracking, managing, and maintaining these configurations to ensure consistency, security, and compliance.

Key Components of Configuration Management:
- **System Configuration**: Ensuring that systems (e.g., servers, endpoints, databases) are configured correctly and securely.
- **Baseline Configurations**: Establishing and maintaining standard configurations for systems and ensuring that all new systems comply with these baselines.
- **Configuration Drift Management**: Detecting and correcting any deviations from the baseline configurations over time (known as "configuration drift").
- **Change Control**: Documenting and controlling all changes made to system configurations to avoid

introducing security vulnerabilities or system failures.

9.1.2: Why is Configuration Management Central to Cybersecurity?

Configuration management forms the foundation of a secure IT environment because it affects nearly every aspect of cybersecurity. Poorly configured systems can lead to vulnerabilities, mismanagement of assets, and weak incident response. For startups and SMBs, effective CM reduces risks and provides consistency across the organization.

Reasons CM is Central:
1. **Security Baseline Enforcement**: Without standardized configurations, it's impossible to ensure that security policies are consistently applied across the organization. CM enforces security baselines (e.g., password policies, encryption settings) across all systems.
2. **Vulnerability Reduction**: Misconfigured systems are a prime target for attackers. Regularly managing and auditing configurations minimizes the likelihood of vulnerabilities.
3. **Change Management**: Documenting changes in configurations helps reduce human error, which is

one of the leading causes of security incidents. It also ensures that changes are tested and validated before being deployed.
4. **Incident Response Efficiency**: When an incident occurs, having consistent configurations makes it easier to identify issues, isolate compromised systems, and recover quickly.
5. **Compliance**: SOC 2, ISO 27001, and other frameworks require organizations to maintain secure configurations and demonstrate their management. CM simplifies audits and compliance reporting by maintaining logs of all configuration changes.

9.2: Creating a Configuration Management Strategy

To effectively manage configurations, startups and SMBs need a well-defined CM strategy that includes policies, tools, and processes. This section outlines the steps to build a practical configuration management strategy for your company.

9.2.1: Steps to Building a Configuration Management Strategy

1. **Define Configuration Baselines**
    - **Baseline Configurations**: Develop standard configurations for your key systems, including security settings, network

configurations, operating systems, and application configurations.
- **Example**: For your web servers, ensure that all unnecessary services are disabled, that the firewall is configured correctly, and that logging is enabled.
- **Tools**: Use tools like **Ansible**, **Chef**, or **Puppet** to automate the enforcement of baseline configurations across systems.

2. **Inventory and Classify Systems**
    - **Asset Inventory**: Ensure all hardware and software assets are tracked and classified. This provides visibility into which systems need to comply with specific configurations.
    - **Example**: Use an asset management tool such as **Lansweeper** or **ManageEngine** to track all IT assets and their configurations.
    - **Connection to CM**: The asset inventory ensures that all devices and systems under CM are identified, enabling consistent policy enforcement.

3. **Establish a Change Management Process**
    - **Change Control**: Implement a formal process for requesting, approving, and documenting changes to system configurations. Every configuration change should be tested before being deployed.

- **Example**: Set up a change control board (even if it's just a small team) to review all significant configuration changes, ensuring that they don't introduce vulnerabilities.
- **Tools**: Use ticketing systems like **Jira** or **ServiceNow** to manage and track change requests.

4. **Monitor for Configuration Drift**
    - **Drift Detection**: Use tools to continuously monitor for unauthorized or accidental changes to configurations. If drift is detected, systems should be restored to their baseline state.
    - **Example**: If a new administrator accidentally disables logging on a database server, drift detection tools should alert the security team to this deviation.
    - **Tools**: Tools like **Tripwire** or **SolarWinds** provide configuration drift monitoring.

5. **Audit Configurations Regularly**
    - **Configuration Audits**: Perform regular audits of system configurations to ensure they adhere to defined baselines. This also helps detect any misconfigurations that could introduce security risks.
    - **Example**: Use an automated auditing tool, such as **Qualys** or **Rapid7 Nexpose**, to

check whether all systems are using secure configurations and have up-to-date patches.

9.2.2: Using Automation to Manage Configurations

For startups and SMBs with limited IT resources, automation is key to implementing and maintaining a strong configuration management program. Automation ensures consistency, reduces manual errors, and streamlines compliance efforts.

Automation Techniques:
- **Configuration as Code (CaC)**: Treat system configurations as code that can be version-controlled, tested, and deployed automatically. Tools like **Ansible, Terraform**, and **Puppet** allow you to define configurations programmatically and apply them across systems.
- **Automated Patch Management**: Integrate patch management into your CM strategy by automatically applying patches to operating systems, applications, and firmware using tools like **WSUS, SCCM**, or cloud-native tools like **AWS Systems Manager**.
- **Automated Auditing**: Automate compliance checks to ensure that systems remain configured according to security policies. Tools like **OpenSCAP** or **Cloud Custodian** provide ongoing auditing and remediation.

9.3: The Relationship Between Configuration Management and Other Key Security Practices

Configuration management is interconnected with several other essential cybersecurity practices. This section explains how CM ties into asset management (AM), access management (AM), patch management (PM), disaster recovery (DR), incident management (IM), and risk management (RM).

9.3.1: Asset Management (AM)

- **How CM Relates to AM**: Asset management tracks all hardware and software used by the organization, while CM ensures that these assets are properly configured and secured. Accurate asset inventories are critical for applying baseline configurations and monitoring for drift.
- **Example**: CM tools use the asset inventory to automatically apply and enforce configurations across all servers, workstations, and network devices.

9.3.2: Access Management (AM)

- **How CM Relates to AM**: Access management controls who can modify system configurations. Without proper access control, unauthorized users

could alter configurations, leading to security gaps. CM ensures that changes are properly authorized and controlled.
- **Example**: Role-based access control (RBAC) ensures that only specific administrators can change system configurations. CM enforces this by logging changes and preventing unauthorized access.

9.3.3: Patch Management (PM)

- **How CM Relates to PM**: Patch management is part of CM because it involves updating system configurations to apply security patches and updates. CM tools automate patching processes and ensure that patches don't introduce configuration drift.
- **Example**: Automating the application of patches to operating systems and applications using tools like **WSUS**, while ensuring that patches adhere to configuration baselines.

9.3.4: Disaster Recovery (DR)

- **How CM Relates to DR**: Configuration management plays a key role in disaster recovery by ensuring that systems can be quickly restored to their baseline configurations after an incident. If a disaster occurs, consistent configurations across

systems ensure faster recovery and reduce downtime.
- **Example**: After a ransomware attack, CM ensures that restored systems are configured securely before they are brought back online, reducing the risk of reinfection.

9.3.5: Incident Management (IM)

- **How CM Relates to IM**: When an incident occurs, configuration management helps security teams quickly assess the state of affected systems, determine if configuration changes contributed to the incident, and restore secure baselines as part of remediation efforts.
- **Example**: If an attacker exploits a misconfiguration, incident response teams can use CM tools to restore the system to its secure baseline configuration.

9.3.6: Risk Management (RM)

- **How CM Relates to RM**: Configuration management is a risk management tool because it reduces the risk of vulnerabilities due to misconfigurations. By maintaining standardized configurations, CM reduces the attack surface and ensures that systems are configured securely.

- **Example**: Regularly applying security configurations (e.g., disabling unnecessary services, closing open ports) reduces the risk of attack and ensures that systems are aligned with the organization's risk tolerance.

9.4: Configuration Management Best Practices for Startups and SMBs

For startups and SMBs, implementing a comprehensive CM strategy may seem overwhelming, but following best practices can help simplify the process and maximize the effectiveness of configuration management.

1. Start with Baseline Configurations
- **Why**: Having a clear, enforceable baseline configuration for each system type ensures that all systems meet security standards from the start.
- **How**: Define baseline configurations for key systems (e.g., servers, laptops, databases) using automation tools like **Chef** or **Puppet** to enforce these settings across all instances.

2. Automate Where Possible
- **Why**: Automation reduces human error and ensures that configurations are applied consistently. It also simplifies compliance reporting by providing audit trails for configuration changes.

- **How**: Use automation tools to deploy configurations, manage patches, and monitor for drift. For example, use **Terraform** to automate infrastructure provisioning and **AWS Systems Manager** to enforce configuration compliance.

3. **Monitor for Configuration Drift**
   - **Why**: Unauthorized or accidental changes can introduce vulnerabilities. Monitoring for drift ensures that deviations from baseline configurations are identified and corrected quickly.
   - **How**: Use drift detection tools like **Tripwire** or **SolarWinds** to continuously monitor configurations and alert administrators to any deviations.

4. **Integrate CM with Security and Compliance**
   - **Why**: CM is essential for maintaining compliance with frameworks like SOC 2 and ISO 27001. Integrating CM with security and compliance programs ensures that configurations remain secure and aligned with regulatory requirements.
   - **How**: Set up automatic compliance checks using tools like **Qualys** or **Cloud Custodian** to ensure configurations meet compliance standards and generate reports for audits.

5. **Regularly Review and Update Configurations**
   - **Why**: As systems evolve and threats change, configurations need to be updated to reflect new security requirements and system changes.

- **How**: Conduct regular configuration reviews to identify outdated settings, vulnerabilities, and necessary updates. Ensure that configuration management policies are aligned with current best practices.

Chapter 10

Understanding Hardening

In this chapter, we focus on **system hardening**, a critical component of cybersecurity for startups and SMBs. Hardening refers to the process of securing systems by reducing their attack surface, removing unnecessary features, and ensuring that all configurations follow security best practices. From physical security to application hardening, this chapter will guide you through various layers of hardening and provide detailed steps for securing key assets in your organization. We will explore hardening techniques for operating systems, applications, security appliances, networks, and more. This chapter ensures that startups and SMBs can implement practical hardening strategies that align with SOC 2 and other compliance frameworks.

10.1: Physical Security – Setting Environment Controls Around Secure and Controlled Locations

10.1.1: What is Physical Security?

Physical security refers to protecting your company's hardware, network infrastructure, and sensitive data from physical threats, such as unauthorized access, theft, and environmental damage (e.g., fires, floods). For startups and SMBs, physical security often involves protecting office spaces, data centers, and the devices used by employees (laptops, servers, etc.).

10.1.2: Key Physical Security Controls

1. **Access Control for Sensitive Areas**:
   - **Best Practice**: Restrict access to areas housing sensitive systems (e.g., servers, network closets, storage rooms). Use electronic key cards, biometric authentication, or physical locks to control access.
   - **Example**: Use a badge-based entry system for the server room and limit access to authorized personnel only.
2. **Video Surveillance**:
   - **Best Practice**: Install surveillance cameras in sensitive areas and review footage

regularly to ensure there's no unauthorized physical access.
- **Example**: Set up cameras at all entry points and in areas housing critical IT infrastructure.
3. **Environmental Controls**:
    - **Best Practice**: Install temperature, humidity, and fire detection systems to protect against environmental threats. Implement backup power systems (e.g., UPS or generators) to ensure critical systems remain operational during power outages.
    - **Example**: Use **Nest Protect** or **Honeywell** environmental sensors to monitor server room temperature and humidity, preventing overheating or damage.

10.2: Operating Systems – Ensuring Patches Are Deployed and Access to Firmware is Locked

10.2.1: OS Hardening

Operating System (OS) hardening involves securing the operating system by removing unnecessary services, applying patches, and implementing security controls to reduce the risk of exploitation.

10.2.2: Key Steps for OS Hardening

1. **Regular Patching and Updates**:
   - **Best Practice**: Keep all operating systems (Windows, Linux, macOS) up-to-date with the latest security patches. Automate the patch management process to ensure patches are applied consistently.
   - **Example**: Use tools like **WSUS** (Windows Server Update Services) for Windows environments or **Ansible** for automated patching in Linux environments.
2. **Disable Unnecessary Services**:
   - **Best Practice**: Identify and disable any unnecessary services or processes that aren't required for your operations. This reduces the attack surface by limiting potential entry points for attackers.
   - **Example**: Disable **RDP** (Remote Desktop Protocol) on Windows servers if it's not required, and remove services like **FTP** or **Telnet**, replacing them with secure alternatives (e.g., SSH, SFTP).
3. **Lock Down Firmware Access**:
   - **Best Practice**: Prevent unauthorized access to the BIOS or UEFI firmware by enabling passwords and ensuring that firmware is up-to-date.

- **Example**: Set BIOS/UEFI passwords on all servers and laptops, and disable booting from external media to prevent unauthorized OS installations.

10.3: Applications – Establishing Rules on Installing Software and Default Configurations

10.3.1: Application Hardening

Application hardening involves securing the applications your business uses by configuring them securely, removing unnecessary features, and limiting access to sensitive functionality.

10.3.2: Key Steps for Application Hardening

1. **Enforce Strong Default Configurations**:
    - **Best Practice**: Ensure that all applications follow secure configuration guidelines, including enforcing strong encryption, enabling logging, and disabling default accounts or unnecessary features.
    - **Example**: For a web application running on Apache, disable the **directory listing** feature, enforce **TLS 1.2 or 1.3**, and configure **SSL/TLS** for secure communication.
2. **Limit Software Installation Privileges**:

- **Best Practice**: Restrict the ability to install software to administrators or authorized personnel only. Prevent users from installing unauthorized or unapproved software, which can introduce vulnerabilities.
- **Example**: Use Group Policy in Windows to restrict software installation privileges to IT staff only.

3. **Apply Application Patches Regularly**:
   - **Best Practice**: Keep all third-party applications up to date with the latest security patches. Automate the patching process where possible to ensure vulnerabilities are patched quickly.
   - **Example**: Use **Patch My PC** or **ManageEngine Patch Manager** to automatically update third-party applications (e.g., browsers, office suites).

10.4: Security Appliances – Ensuring Anti-Virus is Deployed and Any End-Point Protections are Reporting Appropriately

10.4.1: Hardening Security Appliances

Security appliances, such as firewalls, intrusion detection/prevention systems (IDS/IPS), and anti-virus solutions, need to be properly configured and maintained to protect against external and internal threats.

10.4.2: Key Steps for Hardening Security Appliances

1. **Deploy Anti-Virus and Endpoint Protection**:
    - **Best Practice**: Ensure that anti-virus software or endpoint detection and response (EDR) tools are installed on all endpoints and configured to perform regular scans.
    - **Example**: Use **CrowdStrike**, **SentinelOne**, or **Sophos** to deploy EDR solutions that provide continuous monitoring and automated response to threats.
2. **Regularly Update Signatures and Definitions**:
    - **Best Practice**: Keep anti-virus and IPS/IDS signature databases up to date to detect the latest threats.
    - **Example**: Schedule automatic updates for signature databases at least daily, and perform regular scans across all endpoints and servers.
3. **Monitor and Log Endpoint Security**:
    - **Best Practice**: Ensure that endpoint security solutions report to a central logging system or SIEM (Security Information and Event Management) tool to monitor threats and potential security incidents.
    - **Example**: Configure endpoint security solutions to send logs and alerts to **Splunk** or

ELK Stack for real-time threat detection and analysis.

10.5: Networks and Services – Removing Unnecessary Services (e.g., Telnet, FTP) and Enabling Secure Protocols (e.g., SSH, SFTP)

10.5.1: Network Hardening

Network hardening involves securing network infrastructure by removing outdated or insecure services, enabling secure protocols, and configuring network devices to follow security best practices.

10.5.2: Key Steps for Network Hardening

1. **Remove Insecure and Unnecessary Services**:
   - **Best Practice**: Disable legacy protocols like **Telnet, FTP, TFTP,** and **SNMP v1/v2** that are not secure. Replace them with secure alternatives such as **SSH** and **SFTP**.
   - **Example**: Disable Telnet access on routers and switches and use SSH for secure remote administration.
2. **Secure Network Devices**:
   - **Best Practice**: Harden network devices (e.g., routers, firewalls, switches) by implementing access control lists (ACLs), disabling unused

ports, and configuring secure administrative access.
- **Example**: Implement ACLs on your firewall to limit inbound and outbound traffic to only necessary services.

3. **Segment Your Network**:
   - **Best Practice**: Use network segmentation to isolate sensitive systems (e.g., databases, financial systems) from less sensitive parts of the network.
   - **Example**: Use VLANs or software-defined networking (SDN) to segment networks by function (e.g., internal services, guest networks, production environments).

10.6: System Auditing and Monitoring – Enabling Traceability and Monitoring of Events

10.6.1: Auditing and Monitoring

System auditing refers to the practice of continuously monitoring and logging system activities to detect unauthorized actions, misconfigurations, or anomalies.

10.6.2: Key Steps for Auditing and Monitoring

1. **Enable System Logging**:

- **Best Practice**: Enable logging for all critical systems and applications to capture security-relevant events. Ensure that logs are protected from tampering and stored centrally.
- **Example**: Use **syslog** for Linux systems and **Windows Event Log** for Windows systems. Aggregate logs in a centralized logging solution like **Graylog** or **Splunk**.

2. **Set Up Real-Time Alerts for Anomalies**:
    - **Best Practice**: Configure real-time alerts for critical events, such as failed login attempts, configuration changes, or unauthorized access to sensitive data.
    - **Example**: Set up **ELK Stack** to monitor and alert on suspicious activity, such as multiple failed login attempts in a short period.

3. **Regularly Review Audit Logs**:
    - **Best Practice**: Regularly review audit logs to identify unusual patterns or potential incidents that could indicate a security breach.
    - **Example**: Perform weekly log reviews and set up monthly audit reports to identify any potential vulnerabilities or incidents.

10.7: Access Control – Ensuring Default Accounts Are Renamed or Disabled

10.7.1: Access Control Hardening

Access control is a critical part of hardening systems by ensuring that only authorized users can access critical systems and that default accounts are secured or removed.

10.7.2: Key Steps for Access Control Hardening

1. **Rename or Disable Default Accounts**:
   - **Best Practice**: Default accounts (e.g., admin, root) are often targeted by attackers. Rename or disable these accounts to prevent unauthorized access.
   - **Example**: Rename the default **Administrator** account on Windows systems and disable **root** login on Linux servers.
2. **Enforce Strong Password Policies**:
   - **Best Practice**: Enforce strong password requirements (e.g., minimum length, complexity, expiration) and enable multi-factor authentication (MFA) for all administrative accounts.
   - **Example**: Use password management tools like **LastPass** or **1Password** to enforce

strong password policies and MFA for system administrators.

3. **Limit Privileged Access**:
   - **Best Practice**: Use the principle of least privilege to limit access to critical systems and data, ensuring that users only have the permissions they need.
   - **Example**: Use **role-based access control (RBAC)** to restrict administrative privileges to only those users who require them.

10.8: Data Encryption – Encryption Ciphers to Use (e.g., SHA-256)

10.8.1: Data Encryption

Encryption ensures that sensitive data is protected by converting it into an unreadable format unless decrypted by authorized parties. Proper encryption is essential for protecting data at rest and in transit.

10.8.2: Key Steps for Data Encryption

1. **Use Strong Encryption Algorithms**:
   - **Best Practice**: Use strong encryption algorithms such as **AES-256** for data at rest and **TLS 1.2/1.3** for data in transit.

- o **Example**: Encrypt customer data using **AES-256** in databases and enable **TLS 1.3** for securing communication between web servers and clients.
2. **Encrypt Backups**:
    - o **Best Practice**: Ensure that all backups are encrypted to protect against unauthorized access in case of theft or loss.
    - o **Example**: Use tools like **Veeam** or **AWS S3** with built-in encryption features to secure backup data.
3. **Manage Encryption Keys Securely**:
    - o **Best Practice**: Use a secure key management solution to store and rotate encryption keys regularly.
    - o **Example**: Use **AWS KMS** or **Azure Key Vault** for key management, ensuring keys are rotated on a regular schedule.

10.9: Patching and Updates – Ensuring Patches and Updates are Successfully Being Deployed

10.9.1: Patch Management

Patching is the process of applying updates to operating systems, applications, and firmware to fix known vulnerabilities and bugs.

10.9.2: Key Steps for Patch Management

1. **Automate Patch Deployment**:
   - **Best Practice**: Use automated patch management tools to ensure that patches are applied consistently across all systems.
   - **Example**: Use **WSUS** or **SCCM** for Windows systems and **YUM** or **APT** for Linux-based systems to automate patch deployment.
2. **Test Patches Before Deployment**:
   - **Best Practice**: Test patches in a staging environment before deploying them to production systems to avoid compatibility issues or system crashes.
   - **Example**: Set up a testing environment using **Docker** or virtual machines (VMs) to test patches before rolling them out to live systems.

10.10: System Backup – Ensuring Backups are Properly Configured

10.10.1: Backup Strategy

Backups are critical for ensuring business continuity in the event of data loss or system failures. An effective backup strategy involves regular, automated backups and secure storage.

10.10.2: Key Steps for Backup Strategy

1. **Automate Backups**:
    - **Best Practice**: Schedule regular backups of all critical systems and data. Use incremental backups to reduce storage costs and bandwidth requirements.
    - **Example**: Use **Veeam**, **Backblaze**, or **AWS S3** for automated backups with daily incremental and weekly full backups.
2. **Test Backup Restores**:
    - **Best Practice**: Regularly test your backups to ensure that data can be restored quickly in the event of a disaster or ransomware attack.
    - **Example**: Schedule monthly restore tests to verify the integrity and reliability of backup data.

Chapter 11

Our Company Path to Vulnerability Management

In this chapter, we explore how startups and SMBs can establish and manage an effective **vulnerability management program** to identify, prioritize, and mitigate security risks. Vulnerability management is critical for protecting your organization from cyber threats, reducing your attack surface, and ensuring compliance with frameworks like SOC 2. By following a structured approach to identifying vulnerabilities, assessing their risks, and implementing remediation strategies, startups and SMBs can protect their systems from potential exploitation. This chapter will cover key concepts such as attack surfaces, risk management, data classification, incident management, and commercial tools that can simplify vulnerability management.

11.1: Attack Surfaces and Attack Vectors

11.1.1: What is an Attack Surface?

An **attack surface** is the sum of all the entry points where an attacker could gain unauthorized access to your systems. These entry points include hardware, software, network configurations, and even employee accounts. For startups and SMBs, managing the attack surface is crucial for reducing exposure to potential threats.

- **Types of Attack Surfaces**:
    - **Digital Attack Surface**: Includes all internet-facing assets (e.g., web servers, APIs, applications).
    - **Physical Attack Surface**: Physical access to devices and infrastructure (e.g., laptops, data centers).
    - **Human Attack Surface**: Social engineering attacks that target employees (e.g., phishing, weak passwords).

11.1.2: What is an Attack Vector?

An **attack vector** is the method or path that an attacker uses to exploit vulnerabilities in a system. Common attack vectors include phishing, malware, weak passwords, outdated software, and misconfigured networks.

- **Common Attack Vectors**:
    - **Phishing Attacks**: Social engineering attacks that trick users into revealing sensitive information.
    - **Malware**: Malicious software that can exploit vulnerabilities in systems.
    - **Insider Threats**: Employees or contractors who intentionally or unintentionally cause harm.
    - **Unpatched Systems**: Systems that are not updated with the latest security patches.

11.2: Risk Management

11.2.1: Understanding Risk in Vulnerability Management

Risk management is the process of identifying, assessing, and prioritizing risks to your systems based on the likelihood and potential impact of a vulnerability being exploited. Risk management ensures that vulnerabilities are addressed in a way that aligns with the organization's risk tolerance and business objectives.

- **Key Components of Risk Management**:
    - **Risk Identification**: Identify vulnerabilities that pose a threat to your systems.
    - **Risk Assessment**: Evaluate the likelihood and impact of each vulnerability being exploited.

- **Risk Mitigation**: Implement controls to reduce or eliminate the risk (e.g., patching, system updates, monitoring).
- **Risk Acceptance**: For low-impact or low-probability risks, decide whether it's acceptable to leave the vulnerability unmitigated.

11.2.2: Risk-Based Prioritization

A **risk-based approach** to vulnerability management ensures that you focus your resources on addressing the most critical vulnerabilities first. For startups and SMBs, this approach is essential for managing limited security resources.

- **Steps to Risk-Based Prioritization**:
    1. **Identify Critical Assets**: Focus on the systems and data that are most critical to your business (e.g., customer databases, financial systems).
    2. **Assess Vulnerability Severity**: Use vulnerability scoring systems like **CVSS (Common Vulnerability Scoring System)** to assess the severity of identified vulnerabilities.

3. **Calculate Risk**: Combine the likelihood of exploitation with the potential impact to calculate the overall risk score.
4. **Prioritize Fixes**: Prioritize high-risk vulnerabilities that affect critical assets, then address lower-risk issues as resources allow.

11.3: Data Classification

11.3.1: The Role of Data Classification in Vulnerability Management

Data classification is the process of categorizing data based on its sensitivity and criticality to the business. This helps organizations determine which data should be prioritized for protection. In vulnerability management, data classification informs risk assessments by identifying the most sensitive data that could be affected by a vulnerability.

- **Types of Data Classifications**:
    - **Public Data**: Data that can be freely shared without causing harm.
    - **Internal Data**: Data that should only be shared within the organization.
    - **Confidential Data**: Sensitive data that could cause harm if exposed (e.g., customer PII, financial information).

- **Restricted Data**: Highly sensitive data with strict access controls (e.g., trade secrets, healthcare records).

11.3.2: Protecting Classified Data

Once data is classified, appropriate security controls should be applied based on its sensitivity.

- **Example**:
    - **Confidential Data**: Apply strong encryption (e.g., AES-256), enforce access control policies, and monitor access logs.
    - **Restricted Data**: Implement multi-factor authentication (MFA) and restrict access to authorized personnel only.

11.4: Data Retention

11.4.1: Importance of Data Retention in Vulnerability Management

Data retention refers to how long an organization keeps specific types of data. Retaining sensitive data longer than necessary can increase the risk of that data being exposed through vulnerabilities. By managing the retention and deletion of data, organizations can reduce the attack surface and the potential impact of vulnerabilities.

11.4.2: Implementing a Data Retention Policy

- **Steps for Effective Data Retention**:
    1. **Classify Data**: Determine how long different types of data should be retained based on regulatory requirements, business needs, and security risks.
    2. **Automate Data Deletion**: Implement automated processes for securely deleting data once it's no longer needed.
    3. **Monitor Retention Compliance**: Ensure that data retention policies are followed by auditing and monitoring data storage systems.
- **Example**: Set policies to delete customer PII after a specific retention period (e.g., seven years) unless required for regulatory purposes.

11.5: Incident Management

11.5.1: Vulnerability Management and Incident Response

Incident management involves detecting, responding to, and recovering from security incidents. In the context of vulnerability management, having a well-defined incident response plan ensures that vulnerabilities are addressed quickly in the event of an exploitation.

- **Key Elements of an Incident Response Plan**:
    o **Incident Detection**: Continuous monitoring and alerts to detect vulnerabilities being exploited.
    o **Incident Response**: Defined roles and procedures for addressing the vulnerability.
    o **Post-Incident Analysis**: Conducting a root cause analysis to understand how the vulnerability was exploited and how to prevent similar incidents in the future.

11.5.2: Integrating Vulnerability Management with Incident Management

By integrating vulnerability management into the incident management process, organizations can identify vulnerabilities earlier and respond to incidents more effectively.

- **Example**: If a vulnerability is detected during a security incident, the incident response team can work with the vulnerability management team to apply patches and reconfigure systems to prevent further exploitation.

11.6: Business Continuity and Disaster Recovery

11.6.1: The Role of Vulnerability Management in Business Continuity

Business continuity ensures that critical business functions can continue during and after a security incident. **Disaster recovery (DR)** focuses on restoring operations after an incident. Vulnerability management supports business continuity by identifying and mitigating weaknesses that could disrupt operations.

11.6.2: Incorporating Vulnerability Management into DR Plans

To ensure business continuity, vulnerability management should be integrated into disaster recovery planning.

- **Steps**:
    1. **Identify Critical Systems**: Determine which systems are essential for business continuity and prioritize their protection.
    2. **Test Vulnerabilities in DR Scenarios**: Simulate disaster recovery scenarios to identify potential vulnerabilities that could disrupt recovery efforts.
    3. **Implement Backup and Redundancy**: Ensure that backup systems are hardened against vulnerabilities and can be activated if primary systems are compromised.

11.7: Commercial Tools That Can Ease the Burden

For startups and SMBs, implementing a full vulnerability management program from scratch can be overwhelming. However, there are several commercial tools available that simplify vulnerability identification, assessment, and remediation.

11.7.1: Tenable Nessus

Tenable Nessus is a widely-used vulnerability scanning tool that helps organizations identify vulnerabilities in their networks, servers, and applications. I have personally utilized this software tool extensively over an extended period, and it has consistently proven to be both reliable and effective in supporting my needs.

- **Key Features**:
    - Comprehensive vulnerability scanning for on-premises and cloud environments.
    - Automated Compliance Scans like PCI, CIS, FDCC, NIST, etc. This is a great feature that can help us reduce the burden of compliance.
    - Regularly updated vulnerability database to detect the latest threats.
    - Easy-to-use dashboards and reporting for tracking vulnerability status.

- Recommended for Small teams needing automated vulnerability scanning and reporting.

11.7.2: InsightVM by Rapid7

InsightVM provides real-time vulnerability management, analytics, and reporting, enabling organizations to assess and remediate vulnerabilities quickly.

- **Key Features**:
    - Continuous scanning of systems for vulnerabilities.
    - Integration with security and IT teams to prioritize and remediate vulnerabilities.
    - Customizable dashboards to track remediation progress and risk.
    - **Best For**: Organizations that need real-time vulnerability management and collaboration tools.

11.7.3: Qualys VMDR

Qualys Vulnerability Management, Detection, and Response (VMDR) offers an end-to-end solution for identifying, prioritizing, and mitigating vulnerabilities.

- **Key Features**:

- Automated detection and remediation of vulnerabilities across all IT assets.
- Integrated asset inventory to identify systems and software with vulnerabilities.
- Built-in patch management to simplify remediation.
- **Best For**: Organizations seeking a unified platform for vulnerability management, asset discovery, and patching.

11.8: Building a Comprehensive Vulnerability Management Program

By combining vulnerability scanning, risk management, and the use of commercial tools, startups and SMBs can create an effective vulnerability management program that protects their systems and data from threats. Here's how to implement a complete vulnerability management process:

1. **Asset Discovery and Inventory**: Use tools like **Qualys VMDR** or **Nessus** to continuously discover and inventory all IT assets.
2. **Vulnerability Scanning**: Perform regular automated scans using commercial tools to identify new vulnerabilities in your systems.
3. **Risk-Based Prioritization**: Assess the risk of each vulnerability using CVSS scores and prioritize fixes based on the criticality of affected assets.

4. **Patch Management**: Implement automated patching processes to ensure vulnerabilities are fixed quickly.
5. **Continuous Monitoring**: Set up continuous monitoring and alerting for new vulnerabilities using tools like **InsightVM**.
6. **Incident Response Integration**: Ensure that vulnerability management is integrated into your incident response process to address vulnerabilities during security incidents.

Chapter 12

Creating Our Company's Action Plan to Achieve Our Target State

This chapter focuses on developing a clear, actionable **cybersecurity action plan** to move your company from its current state to its **Target Profile** based on the NIST Cybersecurity Framework (CSF) and SOC 2 compliance requirements. For startups and SMBs, an action plan provides a structured approach to implementing the necessary security controls, policies, and procedures to improve their cybersecurity posture. This chapter will guide you through building an inventory of cybersecurity policies, developing Standard Operating Procedures (SOPs), aligning key areas like asset management and access management, and addressing vendor risk and third-party assessments. It will also provide steps for updating existing policies and creating new ones to meet compliance and security objectives.

12.1: Inventory of Cybersecurity Policies

12.1.1: Why an Inventory of Cybersecurity Policies is Crucial

An **inventory of cybersecurity policies** provides an organized list of all the policies your company needs to enforce security controls and ensure compliance with frameworks like SOC 2. These policies guide day-to-day security operations, ensuring that all employees, contractors, and systems follow consistent security practices.

- **Purpose**: A comprehensive inventory allows you to:
    - Identify gaps where policies are missing.
    - Update outdated policies to reflect current best practices.
    - Ensure that all critical areas, such as data protection, access control, and incident management, are covered by formal policies.

12.1.2: Steps for Creating a Policy Inventory

1. **Identify Existing Policies**:
    - Review your current security policies, such as information security, data protection, access control, incident response, and asset management.

- **Example**: You may already have a data privacy policy, but it might need updating to reflect changes in data handling processes.

2. **Categorize Policies by Criticality**:
   - Prioritize policies based on their impact on your security posture and compliance needs. High-priority policies often include those related to data protection, access control, and incident response.

3. **Evaluate for Gaps**:
   - Identify any areas where your organization lacks formal policies. Common gaps for startups and SMBs include vendor risk management, business continuity, and data retention policies.

4. **Align with Compliance Frameworks**:
   - Ensure that your policy inventory aligns with SOC 2 and other relevant frameworks (e.g., NIST, ISO 27001). SOC 2 requires documented policies for key areas like access control, incident response, and data retention.

12.2: Inventory of Policies and SOPs Related to Cybersecurity Assessment

12.2.1: The Role of Standard Operating Procedures (SOPs)

Standard Operating Procedures (SOPs) provide detailed, step-by-step instructions for implementing cybersecurity policies. SOPs ensure that security tasks are performed consistently, regardless of who is executing them, and they are critical for enforcing security controls.

12.2.2: Creating an Inventory of SOPs

1. **Map SOPs to Policies**:
   - Ensure that every policy has a corresponding SOP that details how the policy will be enforced.
   - **Example**: Your access control policy might have an SOP outlining how user access is requested, granted, reviewed, and revoked.
2. **Include Key Areas for SOPs**:
   - **Data Protection**: SOPs should cover how sensitive data is encrypted, stored, and accessed.
   - **Incident Response**: Develop SOPs that guide employees through incident detection, reporting, and resolution.

- **Patch Management**: Include SOPs that detail how patches are applied, tested, and verified.
3. **Review and Update SOPs Regularly**:
    - SOPs should be reviewed periodically to ensure they reflect any changes in technology, processes, or regulatory requirements. This is especially important for growing startups that frequently introduce new tools and processes.

12.3: Information Security Management

12.3.1: Establishing an Information Security Management System (ISMS)

An **Information Security Management System (ISMS)** provides a formal framework for managing information security across your organization. For startups and SMBs, implementing an ISMS helps to ensure that all security efforts are coordinated and that you can meet compliance requirements.

12.3.2: Steps to Establishing an ISMS

1. **Define Roles and Responsibilities**:
    - Assign specific security roles within your organization. These may include a Chief

Information Security Officer (CISO) or security lead, even if this role is combined with other duties in smaller teams.
   - **Example**: Assign an IT manager to oversee patch management and incident response as part of their broader IT responsibilities.
2. **Document and Communicate Security Objectives**:
   - Ensure that everyone in the organization understands the security objectives, which should align with business goals and compliance requirements.
3. **Implement Risk Management Processes**:
   - Regularly assess and document security risks. Implement controls to mitigate those risks, and review them periodically to ensure they remain effective.

12.4: Asset Management

12.4.1: Why Asset Management is Crucial for Cybersecurity

Asset management involves identifying, tracking, and managing all hardware, software, and data assets. It's essential for ensuring that only authorized and properly configured assets are used within your organization.

It is also essential to understand most of the company departments could be involved in Asset Management and why. HR needs to be involved always, as this department's measures like background checks (which are commonly demanded by SOC 2) might be illegal in some countries, so employee measures related to cybersecurity compliance should be differentiated from country to country. Another use case is when a software developer requests a cloud resource, the Asset Management Process needs to make sure this employee has an active HR record in the company, which could be related to a company employee, a third-party vendor, a consultant, etc. Another example of other departments not related to Engineering is Finance, which is involved in Asset Management in the authorization of engineering expenditures like cloud assets, Hardware, SW licensing, etc.

12.4.2: Building a Strong Asset Management Program

1. **Inventory All Assets**:
    - Create a comprehensive inventory of all IT assets, including hardware (servers, laptops), software (applications, operating systems), and data (customer information, internal files).

- **Example**: Use asset management tools like **Lansweeper** or **ManageEngine** to automate asset discovery and tracking.
2. **Classify and Categorize Assets**:
    - Classify assets by their criticality and sensitivity. Prioritize the protection of high-value assets, such as servers storing customer data or systems running critical business applications.
3. **Implement Continuous Monitoring**:
    - Continuously monitor assets for changes in configuration or ownership to ensure that unauthorized devices are not introduced into your network.

12.5: Access Management

12.5.1: Key Principles of Access Management

Access management controls who has access to systems and data. For startups and SMBs, properly managing access to critical systems is essential to preventing unauthorized access and reducing the risk of data breaches.

12.5.2: Implementing Access Controls

1. **Role-Based Access Control (RBAC)**:

- Use RBAC to ensure that employees only have access to the systems and data required for their roles. Implement **least privilege** principles to minimize exposure to sensitive systems.
- **Example**: Developers may need access to code repositories, but they should not have administrative access to production servers unless necessary.

2. **Multi-Factor Authentication (MFA)**:
   - Enforce MFA for all users, especially for accessing critical systems like databases, cloud environments, and administrative interfaces.
   - **Example**: Use MFA tools like **Google Authenticator** or **Duo Security** to add a second layer of authentication for all admin accounts.

3. **Regular Access Reviews**:
   - Conduct regular access reviews to ensure that users' access is still appropriate based on their roles and responsibilities. Remove or modify access when employees change roles or leave the organization.

12.6: Data Classification

12.6.1: Establishing a Data Classification System

Data classification is essential for protecting sensitive information by categorizing it according to its sensitivity level. This ensures that appropriate security controls are applied based on the type of data.

12.6.2: Steps for Implementing Data Classification

1. **Classify Data by Sensitivity**:
   - Establish categories such as **Public**, **Internal**, **Confidential**, and **Restricted** to organize data based on its criticality and sensitivity.
   - **Example**: Customer personally identifiable information (PII) should be classified as **Confidential** and protected with strong encryption.
2. **Apply Appropriate Controls**:
   - Apply security controls based on the classification. For example, **Confidential** data may require encryption and access control, while **Public** data may not require stringent protections.

12.7: Data Retention

12.7.1: Defining a Data Retention Policy

Data retention policies outline how long different types of data should be stored and when they should be deleted. For startups and SMBs, managing data retention reduces the risk of exposure to vulnerabilities and ensures compliance with legal requirements.

12.7.2: Steps to Develop a Data Retention Policy

1. **Identify Data Types**:
    - Identify all types of data stored by your organization (e.g., customer data, financial records, emails) and define retention periods for each category.
    - **Example**: Financial records may need to be retained for seven years, while customer data may be deleted after two years.
2. **Automate Data Deletion**:
    - Implement automated processes to delete data that has reached the end of its retention period, ensuring that sensitive data is not retained longer than necessary.

12.8: Incident Management

12.8.1: Building an Effective Incident Response Plan (IRP)

An **Incident Response Plan (IRP)** provides clear steps for detecting, responding to, and mitigating security incidents. For startups and SMBs, having a formal IRP ensures that security incidents are handled efficiently and effectively.

12.8.2: Steps for Developing an IRP

1. **Define Incident Response Roles**:
   - Assign roles and responsibilities for incident response. These may include an incident commander, forensic investigator, and communications lead.
   - **Example**: A small IT team might assign one person to oversee incident detection and another to manage recovery efforts.
2. **Establish Incident Response Procedures**:
   - Define clear procedures for detecting incidents, triaging them based on severity, and responding quickly to minimize damage.
   - **Example**: Your IRP should outline how to isolate affected systems during a ransomware attack and notify key stakeholders.
3. **Conduct Incident Response Drills**:

- Regularly test your IRP through simulated incident response exercises (e.g., phishing attacks, data breaches) to ensure that your team is prepared to respond in a real scenario.

12.9: Configuration Management

12.9.1: Configuration Management for Secure Systems

Configuration management ensures that all systems are securely configured and maintained according to security baselines. This reduces the risk of misconfigurations that could lead to vulnerabilities.

12.9.2: Implementing Configuration Management

1. **Establish Configuration Baselines**:
    - Define secure baseline configurations for all critical systems, including servers, applications, and network devices.
    - **Example**: Set up a baseline for web servers that disables insecure services and enforces strong encryption settings.
2. **Monitor Configuration Drift**:
    - Continuously monitor systems for deviations from baseline configurations (known as

configuration drift) and automatically correct misconfigurations when detected.
- **Example**: Use tools like **Puppet** or **Ansible** to ensure configurations are consistently applied across all systems.

12.10: Release Management

12.10.1: Managing Secure Software Releases

Release management involves coordinating the deployment of software updates and changes while ensuring that security is maintained throughout the process.

12.10.2: Steps for Secure Release Management

1. **Version Control and Change Management**:
   - Use version control tools like **Git** and implement change management processes to ensure that all software changes are reviewed and tested before deployment.
2. **Security Testing Before Release**:
   - Conduct security testing, such as vulnerability scans and penetration testing, to identify and fix potential security issues before software is released.

12.11: Project Management

12.11.1: Integrating Cybersecurity into Project Management

For startups and SMBs, ensuring that cybersecurity is considered in every project is critical. Whether developing new software, deploying new systems, or expanding operations, cybersecurity should be a priority from the start.

12.11.2: Steps for Cybersecurity-Integrated Project Management

1. **Embed Security Requirements in Project Plans**:
    - Ensure that security requirements are included in the scope of every project. This includes specifying security controls and ensuring that compliance with frameworks like SOC 2 is considered.
2. **Track Security Deliverables**:
    - Assign specific security tasks within project plans and track their completion, ensuring that no project is completed without meeting security standards.

12.12: Understanding How the Company Can Leverage a SOC 2 Report from a Cloud Vendor

12.12.1: Leveraging Third-Party SOC 2 Reports

Many startups and SMBs use cloud vendors to store data or host services. By leveraging a cloud vendor's **SOC 2 report**, you can demonstrate that your organization's data is stored securely and that your vendor complies with SOC 2 principles.

12.12.2: Steps to Utilize Vendor SOC 2 Reports

1. **Request and Review SOC 2 Reports**:
   - Request SOC 2 reports from your cloud vendors and review them to ensure that they cover the relevant Trust Services Criteria (TSCs) your company is responsible for.
   - **Example**: Verify that the vendor's security controls, such as encryption and access management, meet your organization's compliance needs.
2. **Monitor Vendor Compliance**:
   - Regularly review and update vendor SOC 2 reports to ensure that your third-party providers maintain their security and compliance practices.

12.13: Understanding Risk Management from Third-Party Vendors and What to Assess

12.13.1: Managing Vendor Risk

Managing **third-party risk** is essential for ensuring that vendors do not introduce vulnerabilities or compliance risks into your organization. For startups and SMBs, assessing vendor security practices is critical when working with cloud providers, SaaS platforms, and other service providers.

12.13.2: Steps to Assess and Manage Vendor Risk

1. **Perform Due Diligence**:
   - Conduct a thorough security assessment of vendors before engaging with them, including reviewing their compliance certifications (e.g., SOC 2, ISO 27001).
2. **Use Vendor Risk Assessment Tools**:
   - Use tools like **BitSight** or **SecurityScorecard** to monitor your vendors' security posture continuously and receive alerts about potential security issues.

12.14: Updating Current Policies and SOPs

12.14.1: Regular Policy Reviews

Regularly reviewing and updating security policies and SOPs ensures that they remain aligned with current security best practices, technology changes, and regulatory requirements.

12.14.2: Steps for Updating Policies and SOPs

1. **Review Policies Annually**:
   - Set a regular schedule for reviewing policies and SOPs to ensure that they remain effective and relevant to your organization's security needs.
2. **Incorporate Feedback**:
   - Gather feedback from employees and stakeholders who regularly follow these policies to identify areas for improvement.

12.15: Creating New Needed Policies and SOPs

12.15.1: Identifying Gaps

As your business grows or adopts new technologies, you may need to create new policies and SOPs to address emerging security challenges.

12.15.2: Steps to Develop New Policies

1. **Identify New Policy Needs**:
   - Review your business processes to identify areas where new policies are needed, such as cloud security or mobile device management.
2. **Develop and Implement Policies**:
   - Write clear, actionable policies that define how specific security tasks should be handled, and create corresponding SOPs to guide employees through execution.

Chapter 13

Navigating the Most Common Challenges and Tradeoffs to Reach Our Target State Faster

In this chapter, we explore the common challenges that startups and SMBs face when building and improving their cybersecurity programs, especially when aiming to achieve SOC 2 compliance. Limited resources, small teams, and tight budgets can make it difficult to meet compliance requirements while also protecting against cyber threats. This chapter provides practical strategies for overcoming these obstacles, focusing on maximizing available roles, using automation, prioritizing high-risk areas, and leveraging external resources like consultants and cloud services. By understanding and addressing these challenges, startups and SMBs can accelerate their journey to achieving a secure and compliant cybersecurity posture.

13.1: Strategies for Maximizing the Few Roles in Startups and SMBs

13.1.1: Role Compression in Startups and SMBs

In small organizations, employees often wear multiple hats, which can make it difficult to establish a dedicated cybersecurity team. This section explores how startups and SMBs can **maximize the few roles** available to build an effective security strategy while keeping resource constraints in mind.

- **Key Challenges**:
    - Lack of a dedicated security team.
    - Limited personnel available for both day-to-day operations and security initiatives.

13.1.2: Strategies for Maximizing Limited Roles

1. **Combine Security with IT Operations**:
    - In small teams, the IT manager or system administrator often takes on security responsibilities. While this is not ideal, ensuring that basic security tasks, such as patch management, access control, and backups, are integrated into IT operations helps maximize limited resources.
    - **Example**: An IT administrator can manage routine tasks like patching and system hardening as part of their regular duties,

while external consultants are brought in for more complex security audits or incidents.

2. **Develop Cross-Functional Security Champions**:
   o Identify team members in other departments (e.g., development, HR, finance) who can take on additional responsibilities as **security champions**. These individuals can help raise awareness and implement security best practices in their departments.
   o **Example**: A developer can serve as a security champion to ensure that code reviews include security checks and vulnerabilities are addressed early in the development lifecycle.
3. **Leverage Managed Services**:
   o Use managed security service providers (MSSPs) to outsource key security tasks like monitoring, incident response, and vulnerability scanning. This allows small teams to focus on day-to-day operations while external experts handle specialized security functions.

13.2: Role Multiplicity and Cross-Training

13.2.1: The Importance of Cross-Training in Small Teams

Cross-training ensures that multiple team members are familiar with key cybersecurity tasks, allowing for flexibility in the event of staff turnover or during peak workload periods. This is critical for startups and SMBs where resources are already limited.

13.2.2: How to Implement Cross-Training for Cybersecurity

1. **Identify Critical Security Functions**:
   - Start by identifying the most critical security tasks that need to be covered, such as incident response, patch management, and access control.
   - **Example**: If the IT manager is responsible for incident response, ensure that at least one other team member is trained on how to respond to security incidents in their absence.
2. **Develop Cross-Training Programs**:
   - Create simple, documented processes and training sessions to ensure that multiple team members can handle basic cybersecurity tasks.

- **Example**: Train office managers or general operations staff to monitor critical system alerts and escalate issues to the IT lead.
3. **Rotate Responsibilities**:
    - Periodically rotate cybersecurity responsibilities among team members to reinforce cross-training and ensure that tasks are consistently handled.
    - **Example**: Every quarter, rotate patch management duties between two or three team members to ensure they all remain familiar with the process.

13.3: Automation and Tool Utilization

13.3.1: The Role of Automation in Cybersecurity for Startups and SMBs

Automation helps startups and SMBs reduce the manual workload of cybersecurity tasks, enabling small teams to focus on high-priority activities. With limited personnel and resources, automating routine security tasks, such as patch management, monitoring, and reporting, can significantly reduce the operational burden.

13.3.2: Automating Key Cybersecurity Processes

1. **Automated Patch Management**:
    - Use tools like **WSUS, SCCM**, or **Automox** to automatically deploy security patches across all systems, reducing the likelihood of vulnerabilities being exploited due to unpatched software.
    - **Example**: Set up automated patch deployment to ensure that all systems receive the latest security updates on a monthly or bi-weekly basis.
2. **SIEM and Log Management**:
    - Implement a **Security Information and Event Management (SIEM)** solution to automatically collect, analyze, and alert on security logs and events. Tools like **Splunk, ELK Stack**, or **Graylog** can provide real-time monitoring and threat detection.
    - **Example**: Configure your SIEM to automatically alert your IT team of suspicious login attempts or configuration changes.
3. **Automated Vulnerability Scanning**:
    - Use tools like **Tenable Nessus, Qualys VMDR**, or **Rapid7 InsightVM** to regularly scan your infrastructure for vulnerabilities,

providing automated reports on security gaps that need to be addressed.
- **Example**: Schedule weekly vulnerability scans to identify misconfigurations, outdated software, or known vulnerabilities.

13.4: Prioritization and Risk-Based Approach

13.4.1: The Need for Prioritization in Cybersecurity

With limited time and resources, startups and SMBs cannot address every potential security risk. A **risk-based approach** helps prioritize the most critical security tasks by focusing on high-impact vulnerabilities and threats that pose the greatest risk to the business.

13.4.2: Implementing a Risk-Based Approach

1. **Identify Critical Assets**:
   - Focus on the systems, data, and processes that are most important to your business operations and customer trust. Critical assets often include customer databases, financial systems, and intellectual property.
   - **Example**: Prioritize protecting your customer database over less critical internal systems like non-sensitive file storage.
2. **Assess Vulnerability Risk**:

- Evaluate each vulnerability based on its severity and potential impact, using tools like **CVSS** (Common Vulnerability Scoring System). Prioritize fixing vulnerabilities that have a high likelihood of exploitation and a high impact on critical systems.
- **Example**: A vulnerability in a web server exposed to the internet should be prioritized over an internal server that is not directly accessible from outside the network.

3. **Focus on Quick Wins**:
   - Prioritize actions that can quickly reduce risk with minimal effort, such as enabling multi-factor authentication (MFA), updating firewall rules, or applying critical patches.
   - **Example**: Implement MFA across all admin accounts to quickly reduce the risk of account takeovers.

13.5: Outsourcing and Consultants

13.5.1: When to Use Consultants and Outsourcing

For startups and SMBs, outsourcing specific security tasks to external consultants or managed services can be an effective way to access expertise that is not available in-house. This can include vulnerability assessments, penetration testing, or even full security program management.

13.5.2: How to Leverage External Security Expertise

1. **Outsource Complex Security Tasks**:
   o   Use consultants for specialized tasks such as penetration testing, security audits, or incident response. This allows internal teams to focus on day-to-day operations while external experts handle complex security issues.
   o   **Example**: Hire a consultant to perform a penetration test before your SOC 2 audit to identify any vulnerabilities that need to be addressed.
2. **Use Managed Security Service Providers (MSSPs)**:
   o   MSSPs can handle ongoing tasks like network monitoring, threat detection, and incident response, allowing internal teams to focus on business-critical functions.
   o   **Example**: Engage an MSSP to provide 24/7 monitoring of your network and alert you to any potential security incidents.
3. **Engage Fractional or Part-Time CISOs**:
   o   For strategic security leadership without the cost of a full-time CISO, consider hiring a

fractional CISO. This allows you to benefit from executive-level security expertise on a part-time or as-needed basis.
- **Example**: A fractional CISO can help guide your security strategy, ensuring compliance with SOC 2 requirements while helping you build a scalable security program.

13.6: Documentation and Standardization

13.6.1: The Importance of Documentation in Cybersecurity

For startups and SMBs, properly documented security processes and policies are essential for ensuring consistency, especially in the face of limited resources. Documenting security workflows, incident response plans, and configuration standards enables new employees to quickly understand security practices and reduces the risk of human error.

13.6.2: How to Build Effective Documentation

1. **Create Simple, Actionable Policies**:
   - Keep security policies clear, concise, and focused on the most critical areas. Avoid overcomplicating processes that could overwhelm employees.

- **Example**: Write a simple access control policy that specifies who has access to critical systems and how that access is managed and reviewed.

2. **Standardize Key Procedures**:
    - Standardize processes like patch management, vulnerability scanning, and incident response to ensure that they are performed consistently.
    - **Example**: Develop a patch management SOP that includes steps for scheduling patches, testing updates, and documenting successful deployments.

3. **Automate Documentation Updates**:
    - Use tools to automate the process of keeping documentation up to date. This can include change management tools that automatically update security configuration documents when changes are made.
    - **Example**: Use **Confluence** or **Google Docs** for collaborative documentation management, allowing team members to easily update and share the latest security practices.

13.7: Regular Training and Awareness

13.7.1: The Importance of Security Awareness Training

Human error is one of the leading causes of security incidents, especially in small organizations. **Regular security training** ensures that employees are aware of potential threats, such as phishing attacks, and know how to follow security best practices.

13.7.2: Developing an Effective Security Awareness Program

1. **Train Employees on Cyber Hygiene**:
    - Conduct regular training on topics like phishing prevention, secure password management, and recognizing suspicious activity.
    - **Example**: Use tools like **KnowBe4** or **Cofense** to deliver simulated phishing attacks and security awareness training sessions.
2. **Tailor Training to Roles**:
    - Provide role-specific security training to ensure that employees understand how security applies to their specific job functions.
    - **Example**: Developers should receive training on secure coding practices, while

customer support staff should focus on recognizing social engineering attempts.

3. **Measure Training Effectiveness**:
    - Track training participation and use simulated attacks or assessments to measure the effectiveness of your security awareness efforts.
    - **Example**: Conduct phishing simulations to see how employees respond, and use the results to identify areas where additional training is needed.

13.8: Effective Communication and Collaboration

13.8.1: Building a Culture of Security

For startups and SMBs, fostering a **culture of security** is essential for ensuring that everyone in the organization takes responsibility for protecting data and systems. Effective communication and collaboration between departments, such as IT, HR, and development, are key to building this culture.

13.8.2: Fostering Collaboration Across Teams

1. **Incorporate Security into All Projects**:
    - Ensure that security considerations are included in all projects from the start,

whether it's software development, new system deployments, or vendor onboarding.
- **Example**: Make security reviews a standard part of the project planning process, so that teams are thinking about security risks and mitigations from day one.

2. **Encourage Open Communication About Security**:
   - Create an open environment where employees feel comfortable reporting security concerns or potential incidents without fear of blame.
   - **Example**: Establish an internal communication channel (e.g., Slack or Teams) dedicated to cybersecurity updates, reminders, and notifications.

13.9: Scalable Solutions

13.9.1: Implementing Scalable Security Solutions

For startups and SMBs, security solutions must be scalable to support business growth. Choosing tools and practices that can grow with your company ensures that you don't need to completely overhaul your security program as your needs evolve.

13.9.2: Choosing Scalable Solutions

1. **Cloud-Based Security Tools**:
    o Use cloud-based security platforms that can scale easily as your company grows. This includes tools for patch management, endpoint protection, and vulnerability scanning.
    o **Example**: Tools like **CrowdStrike** and **AWS GuardDuty** provide scalable security solutions that adjust to the size of your infrastructure.
2. **Focus on Automation**:
    o As your company grows, manual security tasks become more difficult to manage. Automating security processes like monitoring, patching, and logging ensures that your team can handle increasing complexity.
    o **Example**: Use **Jenkins** or **Ansible** for continuous integration and automated patching as your infrastructure scales.
3. **Leverage Security Frameworks**:
    o Adopting security frameworks like NIST CSF or SOC 2 early on will allow your security program to scale as your company matures, without having to completely redesign it.

- **Example**: Implement SOC 2 security controls and processes that can easily scale to support larger infrastructure and more complex data management requirements as your customer base grows.

Chapter 14

SOC 2 and ISO 27001 Intersections

In this chapter, we explore the intersections between **SOC 2** and **ISO 27001**, two widely recognized information security standards. Both frameworks aim to protect sensitive data and ensure robust security practices, but they differ in structure, focus, and scope. Startups and SMBs working toward compliance with SOC 2 may also benefit from implementing ISO 27001, or vice versa, as both frameworks share common security principles. This chapter will guide you through understanding the overlaps between SOC 2 and ISO 27001, how they complement each other, and practical strategies for aligning your compliance efforts to streamline security management.

14.1: Understanding the Differences Between SOC 2 and ISO 27001

14.1.1: Overview of SOC 2

SOC 2 (System and Organization Controls 2) is an auditing framework developed by the American Institute of CPAs (AICPA) that focuses on five **Trust Services Criteria (TSCs)**: **Security, Availability, Processing Integrity, Confidentiality,** and **Privacy**. SOC 2 compliance is often required by customers or partners in industries such as SaaS, healthcare, and finance, particularly in North America.

- **Key Characteristics**:
    - SOC 2 is a report based on an audit of an organization's security controls.
    - It focuses on how an organization manages data security, availability, and privacy.
    - SOC 2 is flexible, allowing companies to choose the TSCs that are most relevant to their business.

14.1.2: Overview of ISO 27001

ISO 27001 is an international standard for **Information Security Management Systems (ISMS)**, published by the International Organization for Standardization (ISO). It provides a comprehensive framework for establishing, implementing, maintaining, and continually improving an organization's information security management.

- **Key Characteristics**:
    - ISO 27001 requires the establishment of an ISMS, covering a broad range of security policies, processes, and controls.
    - The framework includes risk management, which helps identify and mitigate information security risks.
    - ISO 27001 is recognized globally and is often a requirement for doing business with international partners.

14.1.3: Key Differences Between SOC 2 and ISO 27001

- **Scope**:
    - **SOC 2** focuses on specific systems or services and is often required for organizations offering cloud services or handling sensitive customer data.
    - **ISO 27001** is broader, covering an organization's entire information security management system, including all processes, assets, and controls.
- **Certification vs. Attestation**:
    - **SOC 2** provides an **attestation** report from an independent auditor based on the

implementation and effectiveness of controls.
- **ISO 27001** offers a **certification** after an external auditor verifies that the organization has implemented and is maintaining an ISMS.

- **Flexibility**:
  - **SOC 2** is more flexible, allowing organizations to choose the relevant TSCs and controls based on their business needs.
  - **ISO 27001** requires adherence to a predefined structure and process, including risk assessment and the selection of applicable controls from **Annex A** of the standard.

14.2: Overlapping Security Controls Between SOC 2 and ISO 27001

14.2.1: Common Themes in Both Frameworks

While SOC 2 and ISO 27001 are different in structure, they share several key security principles that make it possible to align and integrate compliance efforts. Both frameworks emphasize:

- **Risk Management**: Identifying, assessing, and mitigating security risks is central to both SOC 2 and ISO 27001. Each framework requires

organizations to establish processes for managing and reducing risks.
- **Access Control**: Both SOC 2 and ISO 27001 require robust access control mechanisms to protect sensitive data, including the use of multi-factor authentication (MFA), least privilege, and regular access reviews.
- **Incident Response**: Having a well-defined incident response process is mandatory under both frameworks. This includes preparing for, detecting, responding to, and recovering from security incidents.
- **Data Protection and Encryption**: Protecting sensitive data through encryption, both at rest and in transit, is a key requirement in both SOC 2 and ISO 27001.
- **Audit Logging and Monitoring**: Logging and monitoring are required to detect and respond to unauthorized activity or potential security breaches. Both frameworks emphasize logging security events and conducting periodic reviews.

14.2.2: Key Control Overlaps

1. **Access Management**:
    - **SOC 2**: Requires access to be controlled based on user roles and responsibilities, using least privilege principles.

- ISO 27001: Control A.9 in **Annex A** requires the organization to ensure that access to information is based on business needs and security principles.

2. **Incident Response**:
    - **SOC 2**: The **Security** and **Availability** criteria require an incident response plan to ensure timely response to security events.
    - **ISO 27001**: Clause **A.16** focuses on information security incident management, requiring processes to be established for detecting and responding to security incidents.

3. **Encryption**:
    - **SOC 2**: Under the **Confidentiality** TSC, organizations must ensure that sensitive data is encrypted both at rest and in transit.
    - **ISO 27001**: Control **A.10** mandates the use of cryptographic controls to protect sensitive information.

4. **Risk Assessment**:
    - **SOC 2**: Requires risk assessment to identify and address risks related to security, availability, and confidentiality of information.
    - **ISO 27001**: Clause **6.1.2** mandates a formal risk assessment process to identify security

risks and determine appropriate mitigation measures.

14.3: Aligning SOC 2 and ISO 27001 Compliance Efforts

14.3.1: Benefits of Aligning SOC 2 and ISO 27001

For startups and SMBs, aligning SOC 2 and ISO 27001 compliance efforts provides several advantages:

- **Efficiency**: Both frameworks share common security controls, so aligning them can reduce the time and effort required to implement and audit security practices.
- **Global Recognition**: SOC 2 is popular in North America, while ISO 27001 is recognized internationally. Achieving compliance with both frameworks can help you expand your business into new markets.
- **Improved Security Posture**: By implementing the rigorous controls of both SOC 2 and ISO 27001, your organization will have a more comprehensive approach to security, which can lead to better protection against cyber threats.

14.3.2: Steps to Align SOC 2 and ISO 27001 Compliance

1. **Map Common Controls**:

- Create a control mapping between SOC 2's TSCs and ISO 27001's Annex A controls. This will allow you to identify areas of overlap and implement controls that satisfy both frameworks.
- **Example**: Align SOC 2's **Confidentiality** criteria with ISO 27001's controls on encryption and data privacy.

2. **Conduct a Joint Risk Assessment**:
   - Perform a unified risk assessment that considers the requirements of both SOC 2 and ISO 27001. This ensures that risks identified are managed in compliance with both frameworks.
   - **Example**: Use the ISO 27001 risk assessment process (Clause 6.1.2) and map it to SOC 2's risk assessment criteria under the **Security** TSC.

3. **Establish a Centralized ISMS**:
   - Implement a centralized ISMS that meets ISO 27001 requirements while incorporating SOC 2 controls. The ISMS will serve as the foundation for documenting and managing all security policies, procedures, and controls.
   - **Example**: Use ISO 27001's ISMS structure to manage incident response, access control,

and data protection, ensuring it also aligns with SOC 2's audit requirements.

4. **Unified Documentation and Reporting**:
   - Use the same documentation and reporting for both SOC 2 and ISO 27001 compliance audits. This includes incident logs, risk assessments, security policies, and audit results.
   - **Example**: When preparing for your SOC 2 audit, use ISO 27001-compliant documentation to streamline the process, ensuring that controls like encryption, access control, and risk management are well-documented.

5. **Integrate Audits Where Possible**:
   - If your organization needs both SOC 2 attestation and ISO 27001 certification, coordinate audits where possible to reduce redundancy. This can include joint internal audits and pre-audit assessments.
   - **Example**: Perform internal security audits that cover both SOC 2 and ISO 27001 controls, preparing your team for external audits without duplicating efforts.

14.4: Practical Example of Combining SOC 2 and ISO 27001

Case Study: SaaS Startup Aligning SOC 2 and ISO 27001

Scenario: A SaaS startup wants to expand its customer base in both North America and Europe. To meet the security requirements of customers in the U.S. and Europe, the company decides to pursue SOC 2 and ISO 27001 simultaneously.

Steps Taken:
1. **Control Mapping**:
    - The startup maps SOC 2's **Security** and **Confidentiality** criteria to ISO 27001's controls for access management, encryption, and incident response.
    - This helps reduce the duplication of work, as controls implemented for ISO 27001 also satisfy SOC 2 requirements.
2. **Unified Risk Management**:
    - A single risk management process is established using ISO 27001's framework, and the findings are applied to SOC 2's risk-related controls.
    - The risk assessment identifies data breaches as a key risk, leading to the implementation of encryption for customer data and multi-

factor authentication for administrative accounts.

3. **Centralized ISMS**:
   o The startup uses an ISMS to manage all security processes, policies, and incident response activities. The ISMS covers both SOC 2 and ISO 27001 requirements, ensuring consistency across audits.
4. **Audit and Certification**:
   o The startup prepares for a combined audit, ensuring that the same security controls are evaluated for both SOC 2 and ISO 27001. This reduces the time and effort required for compliance audits.

Results:

- The startup achieves both SOC 2 attestation and ISO 27001 certification, gaining trust from North American and European customers while reducing the cost and complexity of managing two separate compliance programs.

14.5: Common Pitfalls and How to Avoid Them

14.5.1: Overcomplicating Control Implementation

One common pitfall is overcomplicating the implementation of security controls by treating SOC 2 and ISO 27001 as entirely separate frameworks. To avoid this, focus on identifying common controls and creating unified policies and procedures.

14.5.2: Failing to Align Audits

Another common issue is conducting SOC 2 and ISO 27001 audits separately, which can lead to duplication of effort. Whenever possible, coordinate audits and assessments to streamline the process and reduce costs.

14.5.3: Ignoring Differences in Focus

While there is significant overlap between SOC 2 and ISO 27001, it's important not to overlook their differences. SOC 2 focuses more on specific systems or services, while ISO 27001 takes a broader view of the organization's overall information security management. Ensure that your compliance efforts address both perspectives.

Chapter 15

Checklists and Templates to Get Ready for Audits

In this chapter, we provide practical examples of **checklists** and **templates** to help startups and SMBs prepare for security audits, particularly SOC 2 audits. Preparing for an audit involves documenting security policies, processes, and controls, ensuring they align with the SOC 2 Trust Services Criteria (TSCs). These checklists and templates will guide you through key steps such as reviewing security controls, collecting evidence, and addressing common audit challenges. The chapter will also cover best practices for maintaining ongoing audit readiness and streamlining the compliance process.

15.1: Why Checklists and Templates are Crucial for Audit Preparation

15.1.1: The Role of Checklists in Streamlining Audit Preparation

Checklists ensure that all necessary tasks, controls, and evidence are accounted for during the audit preparation process. For startups and SMBs, checklists provide a step-by-step guide to systematically review and document the policies, procedures, and systems required to demonstrate compliance.

- **Purpose**:
    - Simplify the complex process of audit preparation.
    - Ensure that all critical areas, such as access control, data security, and incident response, are properly documented and audited.
    - Reduce the risk of missing key controls or evidence, which could result in non-compliance.

15.1.2: Benefits of Templates for Audit Preparation

Templates help standardize documentation and reporting, making it easier to communicate with auditors and meet compliance requirements. They provide pre-built structures for policies, risk assessments, incident reports, and other necessary documentation.

- **Purpose**:
    - Provide a consistent format for documenting policies and procedures.
    - Ensure that required information is captured comprehensively, reducing the need for rework.
    - Help quickly produce the necessary evidence for an audit by following standardized templates.

15.2: SOC 2 Audit Readiness Checklist

The following checklist will guide you through preparing for a SOC 2 audit. Each section corresponds to a key area of SOC 2 compliance, ensuring that your organization's controls and documentation align with the Trust Services Criteria (TSCs).

15.2.1: General Readiness Tasks
1. **Define Audit Scope**:
    - Identify which SOC 2 Trust Services Criteria (Security, Availability, Processing Integrity, Confidentiality, Privacy) are relevant to your business.
    - **Example**: A SaaS company might focus on the Security and Availability TSCs due to the nature of its service offerings.

2. **Assign Roles and Responsibilities:**
   o Designate team members responsible for gathering evidence, answering auditor questions, and implementing security controls.
   o **Example**: The IT Manager might be responsible for providing system logs, while the HR Manager oversees employee security training records.
3. **Review and Update Documentation:**
   o Ensure all policies, procedures, and controls are up to date. This includes the information security policy, access control policy, and incident response plan.
   o **Example**: Make sure your security policy reflects the latest protocols for data encryption and user authentication.

15.2.2: Checklist for Each Trust Services Criteria (TSC)

Security TSC Checklist (Required for all SOC 2 Audits)

1. **Access Control:**
   o Verify that access to systems and data is restricted based on user roles and responsibilities.
   o Ensure multi-factor authentication (MFA) is enforced for administrative accounts.

       - **Documentation**: Provide a copy of the access control policy and evidence of regular access reviews.
2. **Encryption**:
       - Ensure that all sensitive data is encrypted both at rest and in transit, using strong encryption algorithms such as AES-256 and TLS 1.2/1.3.
       - **Documentation**: Provide encryption policy and configuration details from your systems and databases.
3. **Security Awareness Training**:
       - Confirm that all employees receive regular security awareness training and phishing simulations.
       - **Documentation**: Provide training schedules, attendance logs, and records of simulated phishing test results.

Availability TSC Checklist

1. **Disaster Recovery and Business Continuity**:
       - Ensure that you have a documented disaster recovery (DR) and business continuity plan (BCP) in place, with evidence of testing these plans.
       - **Documentation**: Provide the disaster recovery plan and test reports from recovery drills.

2. **System Monitoring**:
   o Verify that systems are continuously monitored for uptime and performance, and that alerts are configured to notify the relevant teams of system failures.
   o **Documentation**: Provide evidence of monitoring (e.g., logs from Datadog or AWS CloudWatch) and incident response records.

Confidentiality TSC Checklist

1. **Data Classification and Protection**:
   o Ensure that sensitive data is classified according to its criticality and protected with appropriate controls, such as encryption and access restrictions.
   o **Documentation**: Provide the data classification policy and logs showing how access to sensitive data is monitored and restricted.
2. **Data Retention and Deletion**:
   o Ensure that data is retained and deleted according to your data retention policy, and confirm that data no longer needed is securely deleted.
   o **Documentation**: Provide the data retention policy and evidence of data deletion procedures (e.g., logs showing data removal from backup systems).

15.3: Evidence Collection Template

This template helps organize and track evidence required for an audit, ensuring that you have all the necessary documentation in one place. It can be customized to fit your organization's specific audit needs.

15.3.1: Example of Evidence Collection Table

Control Area	Evidence Description	Owner	Evidence Source	Collected (Y/N)	Notes
Access Control	User access logs (past 6 months)	IT Manager	Active Directory, Okta	Yes	Logs exported to auditor

Encryption	Database encryption configurations	DevOps	AWS RDS Configuration Settings	No	Scheduled for next week
Incident Response	Incident reports for the last 12 months	Security Officer	Incident Response Plan	Yes	All reports submitted
Data Retention	Proof of data deletion for expired records	Data Officer	Backup system logs	No	Awaiting backup logs

Table 3. Example of Evidence Collection Table

15.3.2: How to Use the Template
1. **Identify Control Areas**:
   - Break down the key control areas you need to demonstrate, such as access control,

encryption, incident response, and data retention.
2. **Assign Evidence Collection Owners**:
   - Assign team members responsible for gathering the required evidence for each control area.
3. **Track Evidence Collection**:
   - Use the template to track the status of each evidence item (e.g., collected, pending, or missing) and note any follow-up actions required.

15.4: Policy Templates for Audit Preparation

15.4.1: Access Control Policy Template

Access Control Policy

This policy outlines how access to sensitive data and systems is managed, ensuring that only authorized personnel can access critical resources.

1. **Purpose**:
   - Define the purpose of the policy, which is to protect sensitive data and systems by restricting access based on role and responsibility.
2. **Access Control Mechanisms**:
   - Describe the mechanisms used to control access, such as role-based access control

(RBAC), multi-factor authentication (MFA), and least privilege.
   - **Example**: "All users must authenticate using MFA before accessing the customer database. Administrative accounts are restricted to system administrators only."
3. **Access Reviews**:
   - Specify the frequency of access reviews (e.g., quarterly) and the process for revoking unnecessary access.
   - **Example**: "Quarterly access reviews will be conducted by the IT team to ensure that all access is appropriate and up to date."

15.4.2: Incident Response Plan Template

Incident Response Plan (IRP)

This plan outlines the steps to take when a security incident is detected, including how to contain, investigate, and recover from incidents.

1. **Incident Detection**:
   - Define how security incidents are detected, including monitoring systems, user reports, and automated alerts.
   - **Example**: "Incidents will be detected using SIEM tools, including Splunk and AWS GuardDuty, with alerts sent to the security team for immediate investigation."

2. **Incident Response Team**:
   o Identify the members of the incident response team, their roles, and contact information.
   o **Example**: "The Incident Commander is responsible for coordinating the response, while the IT Lead handles technical remediation."
3. **Incident Response Process**:
   o Detail the steps for responding to an incident, from detection to containment, investigation, and recovery.
   o **Example**: "Upon detection, the affected systems will be isolated, and a root cause analysis will be conducted within 24 hours."

15.5: Ongoing Audit Readiness and Maintenance

15.5.1: Maintaining Continuous Audit Readiness

To ensure continuous audit readiness, startups and SMBs should implement processes to maintain and review security controls regularly. This reduces the risk of being caught unprepared for audits and ensures compliance with evolving security standards.

1. **Continuous Monitoring and Logging**:
   o Set up automated monitoring for key systems and regularly review logs to ensure that

security events are detected and handled promptly.
- **Example**: Use tools like **Splunk** or **Datadog** to continuously monitor security logs and send alerts to the IT team for investigation.

2. **Regular Internal Audits**:
   - Conduct internal security audits on a quarterly or semi-annual basis to ensure that controls are being followed and any gaps are addressed.
   - **Example**: Perform an internal audit of access controls every six months to verify that only authorized users have access to critical systems.

3. **Policy Reviews and Updates**:
   - Schedule regular reviews of security policies and update them to reflect changes in business operations, technology, or regulatory requirements.
   - **Example**: Update your incident response plan annually to reflect any new security tools or team changes.

15.5.2: Preparing for External Audits

1. **Pre-Audit Self-Assessment**:
   - Before your official audit, conduct a pre-audit self-assessment using the checklists

and templates from this chapter to identify any gaps or issues that need to be addressed.
2. **Engage External Auditors Early**:
    - Communicate with your external auditors ahead of time to understand their expectations and ensure that all necessary documentation and evidence are prepared.

Chapter 16

Our SOC 2 Readiness Assessment

In this chapter, we explore the importance of conducting a **Readiness Assessment** to prepare for a SOC 2 audit. A readiness assessment is a pre-audit evaluation that helps identify gaps in your security controls, processes, and documentation before an official audit takes place. For startups and SMBs, performing a readiness assessment allows you to address any deficiencies, align your security practices with SOC 2 requirements, and ensure a smoother audit process. This chapter provides detailed steps for conducting a readiness assessment, choosing the right audit partner, understanding assessment findings, and creating an action plan to address any identified gaps.

16.1: What is a Readiness Assessment?

16.1.1: Purpose of a Readiness Assessment

A **readiness assessment** is a preliminary review of your organization's security controls, policies, and processes to determine whether they meet the requirements for SOC 2 compliance. This assessment helps identify gaps and areas that need improvement before undergoing the formal audit.

- **Goals**:
    - Identify gaps in security controls that could result in non-compliance.
    - Verify that policies, procedures, and documentation align with SOC 2 Trust Services Criteria (TSCs).
    - Ensure that all systems and processes are prepared for an audit.
    - Provide a roadmap for remediation and improvement before the formal SOC 2 audit.

16.1.2: Key Components of a Readiness Assessment

1. **Scope Definition**:
    - Define the scope of the readiness assessment by determining which **Trust Services Criteria (TSCs): Security, Availability, Processing Integrity, Confidentiality, and Privacy**, are relevant to your business.

- **Example**: A cloud service provider may focus on Security and Availability to ensure customer data is protected and services are reliable.

2. **Review of Security Controls**:
   - Assess existing security controls to ensure they meet SOC 2 requirements, including access control, encryption, monitoring, and incident response.
   - **Example**: Evaluate whether access controls are enforced across critical systems using multi-factor authentication (MFA) and least privilege principles.

3. **Policy and Procedure Evaluation**:
   - Review and evaluate all security-related policies and procedures, such as data retention policies, disaster recovery plans, and incident response protocols, to ensure they are documented and up to date.
   - **Example**: Ensure that the incident response plan outlines clear steps for detection, containment, and reporting of security incidents.

4. **Evidence Collection and Documentation**:
   - Identify which documents and evidence need to be collected for the formal audit, such as system logs, employee training records, and access control reports.

- **Example**: Collect logs from your SIEM system (e.g., **Splunk**) to show evidence of monitoring and threat detection.

16.2: How to Find the Best Company to Work With

16.2.1: Criteria for Selecting an Audit Partner

Choosing the right **audit partner** is critical for conducting an effective readiness assessment and achieving SOC 2 compliance. Look for a company that has experience in SOC 2 audits, understands the unique needs of startups and SMBs, and offers guidance throughout the audit process.

1. **SOC 2 Expertise**:
   - Ensure the audit partner has deep knowledge of SOC 2 and has successfully helped similar organizations achieve compliance.
   - **Example**: Ask potential audit firms about their experience working with companies in your industry or of similar size to yours.
2. **Industry-Specific Experience**:
   - Choose a partner familiar with your industry and specific regulatory requirements, such as **HIPAA** for healthcare, **PCI DSS** for payment processing, or **GDPR** for data privacy.

- **Example**: A fintech startup should work with an auditor who has experience in financial services and understands the specific data protection requirements for that sector.

3. **Flexible Approach**:
   - Look for a partner that offers a collaborative and flexible approach, providing support during both the readiness assessment and the formal audit.
   - **Example**: A good audit partner will guide you through remediation steps and help prioritize improvements based on risk and compliance requirements.

4. **Technology and Tools**:
   - The audit partner should use modern tools to automate evidence collection, facilitate communication, and track progress.
   - **Example**: Some audit firms provide tools like **Vanta**, **Drata**, or **Tugboat Logic** to automate evidence collection and simplify the audit preparation process.

16.2.2: Questions to Ask When Evaluating Audit Partners

1. What is your experience with SOC 2 audits?
2. How do you help startups and SMBs with limited resources prepare for audits?

3. What tools do you provide to help streamline the readiness assessment and audit process?
4. Can you provide references from companies of a similar size and industry?
5. Do you offer ongoing support post-assessment to ensure continuous compliance?

16.3: Understanding Our Findings

16.3.1: Analyzing Readiness Assessment Results

Once the readiness assessment is complete, the audit partner will provide a detailed report outlining the findings. Understanding these results is critical for prioritizing remediation efforts and aligning your security practices with SOC 2 requirements.

- **Types of Findings**:
    - **Non-Conformities**: These are areas where your current security practices do not meet SOC 2 requirements and need to be addressed.
    - **Best Practice Recommendations**: These are suggestions for improving your security posture beyond what is strictly required for SOC 2 compliance.

16.3.2: Key Areas to Focus on in Assessment Findings

1. **Control Gaps**:
   - Identify any **control gaps** where security controls are either missing or insufficient. These are critical issues that need to be addressed before the audit.
   - **Example**: A lack of formal access reviews or missing encryption for sensitive data might be flagged as a gap.

2. **Policy Deficiencies**:
   - Review any deficiencies in security policies, such as outdated policies, missing documentation, or policies that are not enforced consistently.
   - **Example**: If the incident response plan is outdated or hasn't been tested in the last year, it will need to be revised and tested.

3. **Documentation Gaps**:
   - Assess whether all required documentation is complete and up to date. This includes evidence like system logs, training records, and risk assessments.
   - **Example**: The readiness assessment may highlight a need for more detailed documentation of backup procedures and testing.

4. **Remediation Timeline**:

- The readiness report should include a recommended timeline for addressing findings, prioritized by risk level and impact on compliance.
- **Example**: Critical security gaps (e.g., lack of encryption for customer data) should be remediated immediately, while lower-priority items (e.g., refining policy language) may be addressed over a longer timeframe.

16.4: Creating an Action Plan

16.4.1: Prioritizing Remediation Tasks

After reviewing the findings of the readiness assessment, the next step is to create an **action plan** that addresses identified gaps and prepares your organization for the formal SOC 2 audit.

- **Steps for Creating an Action Plan**:
  1. **Prioritize Based on Risk**:
     - Focus on high-risk gaps first, such as weak access controls, missing encryption, or unpatched systems. These pose the greatest risk to data security and compliance.
     - **Example**: If access controls are weak and administrative privileges are not

properly restricted, this should be prioritized for immediate action.

2. **Address Policy and Documentation Gaps**:
   - Update or create missing policies and documentation, ensuring they are aligned with SOC 2 requirements. This may include refining the incident response plan, updating the data retention policy, or formalizing risk assessments.
   - **Example**: If your data retention policy doesn't cover secure data deletion, this will need to be updated to ensure sensitive information is properly destroyed when no longer needed.

3. **Set Realistic Deadlines**:
   - Assign deadlines for each remediation task, ensuring they are achievable based on available resources and auditor expectations.
   - **Example**: Set a 30-day deadline for updating encryption configurations on all databases, while allowing 60 days to conduct access reviews and remediate any issues.

4. **Assign Ownership**:

- Assign specific team members or departments responsibility for each remediation task, ensuring accountability and progress tracking.
- **Example**: The IT team may be responsible for implementing access controls, while the HR department might handle employee training and awareness updates.

16.4.2: Tracking Progress and Continuous Improvement

1. **Use Project Management Tools**:
    - Track the progress of your action plan using project management tools like **Trello**, **Asana**, or **Jira**. This helps ensure visibility, accountability, and timely completion of tasks.
    - **Example**: Set up a Trello board to track remediation tasks, assign owners, and monitor deadlines.
2. **Conduct Periodic Reviews**:
    - Schedule regular check-ins with the team to review the status of remediation efforts, address roadblocks, and adjust timelines as necessary.
    - **Example**: Hold weekly or bi-weekly meetings to review progress and ensure that

the most critical tasks are on track for completion before the formal audit.

3. **Prepare for the Formal Audit**:
    o Once all remediation tasks are completed, conduct a final review of all documentation, policies, and evidence to ensure everything is ready for the formal SOC 2 audit.
    o **Example**: Perform a mock audit or self-assessment to simulate the formal audit process and ensure no critical areas have been overlooked.

16.5: Post-Readiness Assessment Best Practices

16.5.1: Maintain Ongoing Compliance

Achieving SOC 2 compliance is not a one-time event; it requires continuous monitoring, review, and improvement to maintain compliance over time.

- **Continuous Monitoring**:
    o Implement continuous monitoring of critical systems to detect and address potential security issues in real-time. Tools like **Datadog, AWS CloudWatch**, or **Splunk** can help monitor system performance, security events, and potential incidents.
- **Regular Policy Updates**:

- Schedule regular updates to key security policies, such as access control, data retention, and incident response. Ensure that any changes to business operations or technology are reflected in your policies.
- **Example**: Update your access control policy whenever new systems are deployed or when new roles and responsibilities are introduced in the organization.

16.5.2: Preparing for the Next Audit Cycle

SOC 2 audits typically occur annually, so it's essential to remain audit-ready throughout the year. By maintaining ongoing compliance and continuously improving your security posture, you can reduce the effort required for subsequent audits.

1. **Perform Periodic Self-Assessments**:
    - Conduct internal audits or self-assessments every six months to ensure that your security controls remain effective and compliant with SOC 2.
    - **Example**: Use the same checklists and templates from Chapter 15 to perform a self-assessment before your next formal audit.
2. **Foster a Culture of Security**:

- Promote security awareness across the organization by providing ongoing security training and encouraging employees to follow best practices.
- **Example**: Hold quarterly security awareness training sessions and send regular security tips to employees.

Chapter 17

Getting Ready for Our SOC 2 Audit

In this final chapter, we focus on how startups and SMBs can prepare for the formal **SOC 2 audit** after completing their readiness assessment. The SOC 2 audit is a comprehensive process that evaluates your company's security practices and ensures they meet the **Trust Services Criteria (TSCs)**. This chapter will cover the essential steps to finalize your preparation, including gathering evidence, coordinating with auditors, responding to audit findings, and maintaining a smooth audit process. By following these steps, you'll ensure that your organization is ready for a successful audit outcome.

17.1: Understanding the SOC 2 Audit Process

17.1.1: The Purpose of a SOC 2 Audit

A **SOC 2 audit** is an independent review of your organization's controls, policies, and procedures to ensure they align with the SOC 2 Trust Services Criteria (TSCs). The audit validates that your security measures are effective in protecting data, ensuring system availability, and safeguarding privacy.

- **Audit Goals**:
    - To verify that your security controls meet the required TSCs.
    - To assess the design and effectiveness of your controls over time.
    - To provide an attestation report that can be shared with customers, partners, and stakeholders.

17.1.2: Types of SOC 2 Reports

There are two types of SOC 2 reports, and selecting the appropriate type depends on your organization's goals and the requirements of your stakeholders.

1. **SOC 2 Type I**:
    - Assesses the **design of controls** at a specific point in time.

- Suitable for organizations that need to demonstrate compliance but have yet to undergo long-term evaluations of control effectiveness.
2. **SOC 2 Type II**:
    - Evaluates the **operating effectiveness** of controls over a period (typically 6 to 12 months).
    - Best for organizations that want to show their controls are consistently applied and functioning effectively over time.

17.2: Final Preparations Before the Audit

17.2.1: Reviewing Readiness Assessment Results

Before proceeding with the audit, review the results from your **readiness assessment**. Ensure that all issues identified have been addressed and that any remaining gaps have been remediated.

- **Checklist for Final Readiness**:
    1. **Policies and Procedures**: Verify that all documentation (policies, SOPs) is current and complete.
    2. **Control Effectiveness**: Ensure that key security controls (e.g., access control, encryption, incident response) have been tested and are functioning as intended.

3. **Evidence Collection**: Confirm that evidence logs, audit trails, and monitoring reports are organized and available for the auditor.

17.2.2: Organizing Evidence and Documentation

Properly organizing and preparing your documentation will streamline the audit process and ensure the auditor can easily access necessary information.

1. **Create a Centralized Document Repository**:
    o Store all audit-related documents (policies, reports, logs) in a shared, secure platform, such as **Google Drive**, **SharePoint**, or a GRC tool like **Vanta** or **Drata**.
2. **Label and Organize by TSCs**:
    o Categorize documents and evidence by Trust Services Criteria (e.g., Security, Availability, Confidentiality), making it easy for auditors to find relevant information.
3. **Ensure Version Control**:
    o Maintain up-to-date versions of policies and logs. Archive outdated versions, but ensure the latest documents are the ones shared with auditors.

17.3: Engaging with Auditors During the Audit

17.3.1: Establishing Communication with Auditors

Effective communication is key to ensuring a smooth audit process. Engage with the auditors early, and provide them with clear, concise, and accurate information.

1. **Schedule a Kickoff Meeting**:
    - Hold an initial meeting to discuss the audit scope, timeline, and any specific questions or concerns the auditors may have.
    - **Example**: Use the kickoff to clarify what evidence needs to be submitted for each Trust Services Criteria and establish key milestones.
2. **Designate a Point of Contact**:
    - Assign a primary point of contact (e.g., IT Manager or Compliance Officer) to coordinate responses to auditor inquiries and evidence submission.
3. **Clarify Expectations**:
    - Ensure both parties agree on timelines, types of evidence required, and any specific testing the auditor will perform (e.g., vulnerability scans, system walkthroughs).

17.3.2: Handling Requests for Additional Information

During the audit, auditors may request more detailed information or clarification. Be prepared to provide prompt and complete responses.

1. **Anticipate Common Requests**:
    - Be ready to provide additional details on security controls, such as incident logs, user access reviews, or encryption configurations.
2. **Respond Quickly and Accurately**:
    - Timely responses keep the audit on track. Make sure to double-check the accuracy of information before sending it to the auditor.
3. **Provide Context for Complex Controls**:
    - For custom or complex systems, provide additional documentation or context to help the auditor understand how your control implementations meet SOC 2 requirements.

17.4: Navigating the Audit Findings and Report

17.4.1: Understanding Audit Findings

Once the audit is completed, the auditor will issue a report detailing **findings** and any recommendations. These findings typically fall into three categories:

1. **Compliant Controls**:

- Areas where your organization meets or exceeds SOC 2 requirements.
2. **Minor Deficiencies**:
    - Areas that need improvement but do not pose a significant risk to compliance. These are typically low-priority fixes.
3. **Non-Compliant Controls**:
    - Areas where controls are missing, incomplete, or ineffective, requiring remediation before achieving full compliance.

17.4.2: Responding to Audit Findings

It's crucial to respond proactively to any deficiencies or non-compliant areas identified in the audit report.

1. **Prioritize Remediation Efforts**:
    - Focus on addressing high-risk findings first, such as gaps in access controls or lack of encryption for sensitive data.
    - **Example**: If a lack of data encryption is flagged, prioritize implementing strong encryption protocols (e.g., AES-256) across all sensitive systems.
2. **Develop a Remediation Plan**:

- Create a plan outlining how you will address each finding, assign responsibilities, and set deadlines for completion.
- **Example**: Your plan might include revising access control policies, automating access reviews, or conducting staff training.

3. **Communicate with the Auditor**:
    - Stay in contact with your auditor to provide updates on your remediation efforts and ask for guidance if needed.
    - **Example**: Once remediation is complete, request the auditor to review your changes and confirm that the issues have been resolved.

17.5: Maintaining Compliance After the Audit

17.5.1: Continuous Monitoring and Improvement

SOC 2 compliance is an ongoing process that requires continuous monitoring and improvement of your security practices. Maintaining audit readiness year-round reduces the pressure of future audits and ensures a consistently secure environment.

1. **Implement Continuous Monitoring Tools**:
    - Use tools like **AWS CloudWatch**, **Splunk**, or **Datadog** to monitor system performance,

detect incidents, and ensure controls remain effective.
2. **Regularly Update Policies and Procedures**:
    o Schedule periodic reviews and updates to all security policies, ensuring they align with evolving business operations and regulatory requirements.
3. **Perform Internal Audits**:
    o Conduct internal audits every six months or annually to ensure controls remain effective and in compliance with SOC 2 requirements.
    o **Example**: Use the same readiness checklists (from Chapter 15) to perform a self-assessment before the next audit.

17.5.2: Preparing for Recertification

SOC 2 audits are typically performed annually, meaning you'll need to maintain compliance and prepare for **recertification**. Start preparing early to make future audits smoother.

1. **Maintain Documentation Continuously**:
    o Keep evidence, logs, and records up to date year-round so you don't have to scramble when the next audit cycle begins.
2. **Stay Ahead of Evolving Threats**:

- o Continuously update your security controls to adapt to new risks and industry best practices.
- o **Example**: Implement new cybersecurity tools (e.g., AI-based threat detection or zero-trust architecture) to enhance security and maintain compliance.

Conclusion

Achieving SOC 2 compliance is no small endeavor, especially for startups and SMBs facing limited resources, time constraints, and the rapidly evolving landscape of cybersecurity threats. I understand the unique challenges you're up against because this journey isn't simply about meeting checkboxes; it's about building trust with your customers, protecting your organization's data, strategizing around compliance, and creating a sustainable, secure foundation for growth. By following the structured roadmap in this book, you now have the knowledge, tools, and strategies to make this possible, and to succeed in your goals.

From understanding the fundamentals of SOC 2 and exploring the NIST CSF 2.0 framework, to conducting gap analyses and preparing for audits, each chapter has equipped you with a practical approach tailored to your specific needs. The goal wasn't just to provide you with compliance checklists but to help you think critically about security and risk management in a way that supports your long-term success. The Current and Target Profiles you've developed using NIST CSF 2.0 provide a clear path to aligning with SOC 2 requirements while addressing the unique cybersecurity needs of your business. And by implementing your gap-closing action plans, you're not only building a foundation for SOC 2 compliance but creating a resilient cybersecurity program that will scale as your company grows.

Building a security program may seem overwhelming, especially when cybersecurity might not be your primary business focus. But know that taking it one step at a time, starting with what you have and improving incrementally, will get you where you need to go. Each small improvement, each security control added, and every process formalized brings you closer to creating a robust security culture and, ultimately, peace of mind for your customers, partners, and stakeholders.

As you continue on this path, remember that compliance isn't a one-time milestone but a journey. The best cybersecurity programs are those that adapt and grow, just like your business. Keeping up with evolving security threats, updating policies, and monitoring for continuous compliance are steps that will help protect your organization over the long term. With the SOC 2 framework as your guide and NIST CSF as your toolset, you're positioned to make strategic, informed decisions about your security posture, regardless of what lies ahead.

Thank you for allowing this book to be part of your journey. By following these steps, you've shown commitment not just to compliance but to the security and integrity of your organization. Trust that your hard work will pay off, both in achieving compliance and in building a reputation as a trustworthy, secure business. You have the foundation you need to succeed in your goals, and I am confident that, equipped with these strategies, you are ready to tackle the challenges ahead.

Your path to cybersecurity excellence is just beginning, embrace it, build on it, and know that you are prepared for success.

Bibliography

1. American Institute of Certified Public Accountants (AICPA). (2018). *SOC 2® - SOC for Service Organizations: Trust Services Criteria*. AICPA. Retrieved from https://www.aicpa.org/soc2
2. International Organization for Standardization (ISO). (2013). *ISO/IEC 27001:2013 - Information technology - Security techniques - Information security management systems - Requirements*. ISO. Retrieved from https://www.iso.org/standard/54534.html
3. National Institute of Standards and Technology. (2024). The NIST Cybersecurity Framework (CSF) 2.0. doi:10.6028/nist.cswp.29
4. National Institute of Standards and Technology (NIST). (2018). *Framework for Improving Critical Infrastructure Cybersecurity* (Version 1.1). NIST. Retrieved from https://www.nist.gov/cyberframework
5. National Institute of Standards and Technology (NIST). (2020). *Security and Privacy Controls for Information Systems and Organizations* (NIST Special Publication 800-53, Revision 5). NIST. Retrieved from https://csrc.nist.gov/publications/detail/sp/800-53-rev-5/final
6. National Institute of Standards and Technology (NIST). (2022). *NIST Quick Start Guide (QSG) for Cybersecurity*

Framework 2.0 (Draft). NIST. Retrieved from https://www.nist.gov/news-events/news/2022/08/nist-cybersecurity-framework-csf-20-draft

7. Tugboat Logic. (n.d.). *SOC 2 Readiness Checklist*. Tugboat Logic. Retrieved from https://www.tugboatlogic.com/soc-2-readiness-checklist

8. **Center for Internet Security (CIS).** (2021). *CIS Controls v8*. CIS. Retrieved from https://www.cisecurity.org/controls/cis-controls-list

9. European Union Agency for Cybersecurity (ENISA). (2021). *Guidelines on Assessing Security Requirements*. ENISA. Retrieved from https://www.enisa.europa.eu/publications/guidelines-on-assessing-security-requirements

10. International Organization for Standardization (ISO). (2013). *ISO/IEC 27002:2013 - Information technology - Security techniques - Code of practice for information security controls*. ISO. Retrieved from https://www.iso.org/standard/54533.html

11. International Organization for Standardization (ISO). (2022). *ISO/IEC 27005:2022 - Information security, cybersecurity, and privacy protection — Information security risk management*. ISO. Retrieved from https://www.iso.org/standard/80512.html

12. National Institute of Standards and Technology (NIST). (2014). *Framework for Improving Critical Infrastructure Cybersecurity* (Version 1.0). NIST. Retrieved from https://www.nist.gov/cyberframework

13. National Institute of Standards and Technology (NIST). (2020). *Zero Trust Architecture* (NIST Special Publication 800-207). NIST. Retrieved from https://csrc.nist.gov/publications/detail/sp/800-207/final
14. National Institute of Standards and Technology (NIST). (2016). *Guide for Applying the Risk Management Framework to Federal Information Systems* (NIST Special Publication 800-37, Revision 1). NIST. Retrieved from https://csrc.nist.gov/publications/detail/sp/800-37/rev-1/final
15. National Institute of Standards and Technology (NIST). (2018). *Risk Management Framework for Information Systems and Organizations* (NIST Special Publication 800-37, Revision 2). NIST. Retrieved from https://csrc.nist.gov/publications/detail/sp/800-37/rev-2/final
16. National Institute of Standards and Technology (NIST). (2012). *Guide for Conducting Risk Assessments* (NIST Special Publication 800-30, Revision 1). NIST. Retrieved from https://csrc.nist.gov/publications/detail/sp/800-30/rev-1/final
17. Payment Card Industry Security Standards Council (PCI SSC). (2018). *Payment Card Industry Data Security Standard (PCI DSS) v3.2.1*. PCI Security Standards Council. Retrieved from: https://www.pcisecuritystandards.org/document_library

18. American Institute of CPAs. (2014) SOC 1® report SOC 2® report SOC 3® report service organization control reports, AICPA SERVICE ORGANIZATION CONTROL REPORTS. Retrieved from: https://us.aicpa.org/content/dam/aicpa/interestareas/frc/assuranceadvisoryservices/downloadabledocuments/soc_reports_flyer_final.pdf

www.ingramcontent.com/pod-product-compliance
Lightning Source LLC
Chambersburg PA
CBHW052311220526
45472CB00001B/70